Small Bibles for Bad Times

Selected Poems & Prose

LILIANE ATLAN

Small Bibles for Bad Times

Selected Poems & Prose

Translated from the French by
Marguerite Feitlowitz

MANDEL VILAR PRESS, SIMSBURY, CONNECTICUT
DRYAD PRESS, WASHINGTON, D.C.

Small Bibles for Bad Times: Selected Poetry and Prose
English translation and introduction © 2021 by Marguerite Feitlowitz

All rights reserved. No portion of this book may be reproduced in any form or by any means, including electronic storage and retrieval systems, except by explicit prior written permission of the publisher. Brief passages may be excerpted for review and critical purposes.

This book is typeset in Minion Pro, 11 on 15 for text, Avenir Next for heads
Book and cover design by Sandy Rodgers
Cover art, "No Place Like It" by Mindy Weisel
Photographs courtesy of the Estate of Liliane Atlan

Library of Congress Cataloging-in-Publication Data

Names: Atlan, Liliane, 1932-2011, author. | Feitlowitz, Marguerite, translator.
Title: Small bibles for bad times : selected poems and prose / Liliane Atlan ; translated, from the French by Marguerite Feitlowitz.
Description: Simsbury, Connecticut ; Washington, DC : Mandel Vilar Press ; Dryad Press, [2020]
Identifiers: LCCN 2020018205 (print) | LCCN 2020018206 (ebook) | ISBN 9781942134688 (paperback) | ISBN 9781942134701 (ebook)
Subjects: LCSH: Atlan, Liliane, 1932-2011--Translations into English.
Classification: LCC PQ2661.T74 A2 2020 (print) | LCC PQ2661.T74 (ebook) DDC 843/.914--dc23
LC record available at https://lccn.loc.gov/2020018205
LC ebook record available at https://lccn.loc.gov/2020018206

Mandel Vilar Press / 19 Oxford Court, Simsbury, Connecticut 06070
www.mvpublishers.org / www.americasforconservation.org
Dryad Press / 15 Sherman Avenue, Takoma Park, Maryland 20912
www.dryadpress.com

Acknowledgments

Excerpts from the memoir *Petites bibles pour mauvais temps* (2001) used with permission from the publisher L'Harmattan. Poems from *Bonheur, mais sur quel ton te le dire* (1996); *Quelques pages arrachées au grand livre des rêves* in the collection *Ecritures* (1999); and *Peuples d'argile, forêts d'étoiles* (2000) used with permission from the publisher L'Harmattan, (2000). *Le maître-mur*, originally published under the pseudonym *Galil*, éditions alluvions (1958); *Action poétique* (1962); and in a revised and enlarged edition by Dumerchez (2004).

InTranslation@BrooklynRail.com gave early support to this project, in May 2015, by publishing "Water of Memory," "The Train that Crumbled Away," "While I Called out for a Miracle," "Star Forests," "A Wondrous Being Lives Inanimate Within Us," "Based on the Evidence," "Everything Will BeLike Here," "My Death and I: A Song," "These Labors Imposed on my Heart," "Hotel for the Dead: A Dream," "Dead, I Speak to All My Friends."

Exchanges: Journal of Literary Translation (exchanges@uiowa.edu) published "Shawl for the Ends of Life," "Study," and "As One Would Chisel Diamonds," Fall 2018.

We thank the editors for their kind permission to reprint. We should add that some of these poems have been revised for *Small Bibles for Bad Times*.

*I owe my association with Liliane Atlan to my mentor
James Leverett, to whom I dedicate this translation
with love and devotion*

Contents

"Everything Lived Within Me": The Writing of
Liliane Atlan 3

PROSE 11
from *Petites bibles pour les mauvais temps*
from *Small Bibles in Bad Times* 13

POÉSIE
POETRY 47
from *Bonheur, mais sur quel ton te le dire*
from *Happiness, But in What Tone to Tell You* 49

  La morte raconte
  The Dead Woman Recounts 51

  Le maître des marionnettes
  The Master of Marionettes 53

  Je vois des flammes
  I See Flames 57

  Tu es tout, tu n'es rien
  You Are Everything, You Are Nothing 59

  Même seule dans sa maison elle se sentait habitée
  Even Alone in Her House She Felt Inhabited 61

from *Quelques pages arrachées au grand livre des rêves*
from *Some Pages Torn from the Great Book of Dreams* 63

  Le rêve de la salle d'études
  The Dream of the Study Hall 65

  Le rêve de l'étoile enfant
  The Dream of the Star-Child 67

Le rêve de l'oubli The Dream of Oblivion	69
Le rêve des bols pleins de lumière The Dream of the Bowls Full of Light	71
Le rêve des mains The Dream of the Hands	73
Le rêve des bébés The Dream of Babies	75
Le rêve du torrent de lumière The Dream of the Torrent of Light	77
Le rêve de la morte fatiguée d'être seule The Dream of the Dead Woman Tired of Being Alone	79
from Le maître-mur from The Master-Wall	81
Les rats en fête sur l'autel Rats Feasting On the Altar	83
J'ai vu la mort pleurer I Saw Death Weeping	85
La petite voiture de flammes et de voix The Chariot of Flames and Voices	87
Peuples d'argile, forêts d'étoiles As One Would Chisel Diamonds	89
L'eau de mémoire The Water of Memory	91
Forêts d'étoiles Star Forests	93
La douleur anonyme au soleil rayonnait The Anonymous Sorrow Shining on the Sun	95

Constat
Based on the Evidence 97

Tout sera comme ici mais ce sera vivable
Everything Will Be Like Here but It Will Be Livable 99

Le tram qui s'effritait
The Tram That Crumbled Away 101

Au milieu d'une foule oubliée
In the Middle of a Forgotten Heap 103

Le temps que je crie au miracle
While I Called Out for a Miracle 105

Le bracelet de la lumière noire
The Bracelet of Black Light 107

Ces travaux que l'on fait dans mon cœur
These Labors Imposed on My Heart 109

... J'ai traversé les zones noires de la résurrection ...
... I have crossed the black zones of resurrection 111

La lumière oubliée de nos premières heures
The Forgotten Light of Our First Hours 113

Je porte un nom de poussière
I Bear a Name Made of Dust 115

Celui dont je garde le nom secret
He Whose Name I Keep Secret 117

Le scintillement du sable à l'infini
The Sparkle of Sand for Eternity 119

On ne peut vivre seul on ne peut vivre inhabité
One Cannot Live Alone One Cannot Live Uninhabited 121

Ma mort et moi: chanson
My Death and I: A Song 123

Tu me rendais vivante
You Brought Me Back to Life — 127

Le dire sur le ton d'une douleur gaie
Tell It with a Joking Sorrow — 129

Le châle des fins de vie
Shawl for the Ends of Life — 131

Si la résurrection des morts n'est pas un canular
If the Resurrection of the Dead Is Not a Scam — 133

L'étude
Study — 135

Le rêve de l'hôtel des morts
Hotel for the Dead: A Dream — 137

Peuples d'argile
People of Clay — 139

Le son de l'âme qui me traverse
The Sound of the Soul Passing through Me — 141

Comme on cisèlerait des diamants
As One Would Chisel Diamonds — 143

Adieu posthume de Liliane
Liliane's Posthumous Adieu — 145

Morte, je parle, à tous mes amis
Dead, I speak, to all my friends — 147

On Translating Liliane Atlan — 149

Translator's Acknowledgments — 155

"Everything Lived Within Me": The Writing of Liliane Atlan

For Liliane Atlan (1932-2011), French writer of plays, poetry, and prose, the creative quest was to "find language to say the unsayable... to [find a way] to integrate within our conscience, without dying in the attempt, the shattering experience of Auschwitz."[1] In 1939, just before the German Occupation of France, seven-year-old Liliane and her sister Rachel were sent into hiding with a gentile family in the Auvergne. As Atlan has recounted, this would be the wellspring for her writing.

> We had to entertain ourselves. My sister would dress up, would disguise herself. She was the audience. I was the stage: the actors, the author.... Everything lived within me: I screamed, gesticulated, died. I would speak out my lamentations, my dirges, my psalms. After the war nothing seemed possible. There was no way out for us. Man and his gods had died in the concentration camps.[2]

During the war, their mother, the formidable Marguerite Beressi, managed to run the family business, while their father, Elie Cohen, fought in the French army. Originally from Salonica, Greece — whose ancient Jewish community was decimated by the Nazis — Elie Cohen helped fellow Jews evade the Nazis, and personally provided relief and resources to refugees and survivors after the war. Once the family were reunited in Montpellier, the adults undertook an anguished search for their missing relatives, a process that in itself was traumatizing for the young Liliane. They soon learned that Atlan's maternal grandmother and uncles all died in Auschwitz. Elie Cohen was intent, maybe obsessed, with helping others, and their home became his base of operation. Liliane recounted to me (and others) the shock of returning from school to find a girl not much older than herself — skeletal, her head still shaved, her eyes dead — waiting to be taken to her next provisional home. Another time, she came home to find a pianist who had been made to play music as her daughter was being led to the gas chamber in Auschwitz. Still horrified and ashamed of her own reaction many years later, Atlan told me that she ran to the bathroom to vomit. Not long afterward, she became extremely ill. "Almost as a reflex," as Liliane once put it, "I stopped eating," unable to withstand the continual recounting of round-ups, torture, death camps, and killing. In desperation, her parents would eventually send her to a clinic in Switzerland. What others called anorexia, she would later denominate as a symptom of le mal de terre, "earth sickness," an abiding theme in her work, and a recurrent subtitle.

Everything lived within me — Liliane was, to an extreme degree, porous in the way she watched and listened to others. In 1947, a nineteen-year-old survivor of Auschwitz, who had lost his whole family there, became, for all intents and purposes, part of the Cohen family. ("The only reason I didn't let them legally adopt me was that I didn't want to change my name," said Bernard Khul many years later.) Traumatized, solitary, and all but mute, Khul had tried to starve himself to death in a Paris hotel room. He was slowly brought back to social living by the kind patience of the Cohens. "I told Liliane, who by that time was no more than fourteen, more than I ever told anyone, including my own children. She just kept asking me, asking questions, and listened so intently." The bond with Bernard Khul was lifelong. As he recounts, she sent him every text she wrote before it was published, always asking his opinion. "Such unusual writing, unlike what one had ever read, but beautiful. In the theatre, at the end of her plays, there was usually silence — the audience would be stunned, these were plays like no other, terrifying, disruptive of rational thinking, but so beautiful, language like the rarest poetry." For her part, Atlan insisted, "That I'm able to write, what I write, is thanks to Bernard and the things he told me."[3]

After treatment in Switzerland, Atlan passed her Baccalaureate and entered the Sorbonne to study Philosophy; she would later complete her graduate thesis under the direction of Gaston Bachelard, writing on "The Arbitrary and the Fantastical in Nietzsche." In 1948, Atlan started attending the extremely selective Gilbert Bloch d'Orsay School founded in 1946 by heroes of the Jewish Resistance for youths traumatized by the Shoah.[4] Friends from that time believe the school saved her, physically, mentally and spiritually. Here, she studied Talmud, Torah, mystical texts, as well as Jewish history, in a cohort that included future luminaries in academe, science, theology, and literature. In *Small Bibles for Bad Times* (excerpted in this volume) the school is dubbed "I Study." It was here that Liliane Cohen met the fellow student she would marry in 1952, Henri Atlan, who would become a pioneering biophysicist, neuroscientist, and philosopher. The school fashioned itself as a "Jewish Polytech," combining orthodox practice, modern inquiry, and science; sophisticated textual analyses; and intense theological, philosophical, and political debate. It's perhaps hard to believe, but some delightful comedy is found in these pages "for bad times." Liliane's father is dubbed God's Not Doing His Job, I'm Replacing Him; her husband is I Will Discover the Secret of Life; she herself is No, But I'll Get Out of This.

While Atlan is known for her plays,[5] her extensive non-theatrical works make up an important part of her oeuvre. The poems and prose here are published in English for the first time, and were selected to display her technical range, and to demonstrate that her "small" texts, individually and together, carry a great deal of weight.

In virtually all of her work, the mundane and cosmic, devotional and defiant, lyric and political jostle, subvert, and re-create each other. Atlan defies easy categorization: she's "a "Jewish writer," "a Holocaust writer," an originator of l'écriture féminine, and a pioneering theatre artist, one of the first (in the early 1980s) to experiment with video, sound, and

 spatial technology to link, even layer, performances of her plays. Her writing is steeped in her learned agon with Torah, Talmud, and Kabblah, and her French is inflected with Hebrew, Ladino, and Yiddish.

Atlan was catapulted into prominence in 1967 with the production of her first play, the surreal *Monsieur Fugue*, inspired by Janusz Korszak, the Polish educator, radio artist, and orphanage director who voluntarily accompanied a group of children from the Warsaw Ghetto to Auschwitz. Atlan turns this instance of mythic altruism into a story that's even more shocking: it's not Korszak but a Nazi soldier, crazed by all he's seen and done, who "turns," who wants to be among the doomed children in the truck to "Rotburg" (Auschwitz). On the way, the children (who have been living in a sewer and are also crazed, and capable of great cruelty and violence) act out the lives they would have lived were they not imminently to die. The children age before our eyes, fighting through life, raging against and ultimately accepting death as old men and women. First performed at the Comédie de St. Etienne, under the direction of Roland Monod, *Monsieur Fugue* was reprised at the Festival d'Avignon (which would premiere a number of Atlan's later plays), and soon after, in Israel. The play won major prizes in Europe and Israel, and is regularly performed.[6]

In 1969, Liliane and Henri Atlan, and their two children, went to live in Israel, where they stayed until 1971. As she recounts in the excerpt from *Small Bibles for Bad Times*, she began (not always successfully) to make street theatre with Palestinian artists. Until her death, in Israel, in 2011, Atlan, recipient of the Prix Mémoire de la Shoah among other prestigious awards for Jewish writers, was active in Israeli-Palestinian peace and cultural initiatives.

6

Much of Atlan's work pre-figures and/or embodies trauma theory, and investigations into sex and gender. This is writing rooted in the body, enflamed by empathy, and informed by a life of rarefied study. In the late 1960s, Atlan lived in San Francisco, where she was introduced to new forms of collective theatre creation based on improvisation among actors in rehearsal and with the audience during public performances. Back in Paris, Atlan would employ these techniques in pioneering treatment programs for drug addiction: first in 1975 for addicts in post-withdrawal; and then in 1976 at the Centre Médical Marmottan for in-patients. She began using video as a means to document patient testimonies and improvisations, and then as a creative tool to layer and configure them in collectively-made theatre pieces. *Even Birds Can't Always Get High* (*Même les oiseaux ne peuvent pas toujours planer*) arose from her work with recovering addicts; its title comes from a healing tale by the Hasidic Rabbi Nachman of Breslov (1772-1810), about birds born with an infirmity that makes it impossible for them to fly.

While plays are absent from this volume, dramatic elements abound: scenes and vignettes; scoring for voices; desires, plots and characters engaged in mortal conflict, sometimes within a single mind. Especially in the poems, much depends on cadence, breath, and beat. Ritual is interrogated even as it's performed; conventional wisdoms are discarded, mocked and mutilated; study is sacred, belief suspect, genuine lessons exist to be learned the hard way. Phrases are shorn of ballast, words are dug down to their roots, images are so precise and searing that, while often shocking, they yet have the solidity of fact, as in these two prose poems:

> Waves, hateful waves, were staring through me. With her bare hands, a peasant woman parted them, held them up toward the sky while I called out for a miracle, then she let them become snakes.

> I was in a tram made of earth, which struggled on the steep slopes above the void, not stopping, transporting no one but me, crumbling away to

nothing by the time it abandoned me, near a sort of haven lost in a vast emptiness.

There is no escape from history, no sidestepping the battle with God or with patriarchal religious authorities; no ready acquiescence to received notions of virtue, order, or even justice. Characters, images, and elements recur in the texts here — but from different angles, in different frames and genres, and to different ends. The effect is rather like that of kaleidoscope, with visions that return, somehow changed by the ways in which we've looked at them before.

Atlan's poems have the disquieting elegance and musicality of Pizarnik; they are resonant with history; and have a sidelong humor and sudden tenderness that calls up Lispector. The cohabitation, in Atlan, of the mythic and the mundane makes me think of the poems of French-Lebanese Vénus Khoury-Ghata.[7]

This volume brings me full circle to my first book, a collection of three of Liliane's plays, edited by Bettina Knapp. Liliane and I first met, in the mid-1980s, on a blustery spring evening in Manhattan. After leaving Bettina's beautiful, art-filled apartment on the Upper West side, Liliane turned me and, said, in her lovely if peremptory French, "Take me to CBGB," as though I (then in my twenties) went there every night. In fact, the night before, I'd been to a classical concert at Carnegie Hall, which I don't think I had the nerve to mention. CBGB was the first punk rock club, located in the scruffy East Village. Liliane was only too happy to plunge down into the subway, climb back up a stairwell that smelled of urine and come out on trash-strewn Second Avenue. She seemed disappointed that CBGB wasn't wilder (it was a week-night); but we stayed for hours, our ears ringing, and our guts burning from lousy red wine. She tried to persuade me to walk all night but (alas) I had a job I needed to show up for in the morning. That was Liliane, as everyone who knew her maintains: she was surprising, unsettling, and fascinating; questing, affectionate and demanding; fun, but also full of anguish.

As One Would Chisel Diamonds, included in full, is her final, and I think most beautiful book. Liliane seemed to know it would be her last. It is possessed of generosity, wit, and gratitude. And the writing is effervescent.

— Marguerite Feitlowitz
Bennington, Vermont

Notes

[1] Over the years that I knew Liliane, she made these statements with myriad small variations. See Judith Morganroth Schneider, "Liliane Atlan," Jewish Women's Archive, A Comprehensive Historical Encyclopedia (jwa.org/encyclopedia/article-atlan-liliane). See also www.lilianeatlan.com, the website created and actively curated by Liliane's children, Michaël Atlan and Miri Keren; there are excerpts from Liliane's work, interviews with her and her creative collaborators (Roland Monod, J.J. Grumberg, et al), and friends, as well as a solid and up-to-date bibliography.

[2] Bettina L. Knapp, Introduction, *Theatre Pieces: An Anthology by Liliane Atlan*, translated by Marguerite Feitlowitz, Greenwood, Florida: The Penkevill Publishing Co., 1985, 2. Knapp had originally included this anecdote in her *Off-Stage Voices*, Troy: New York, The Whitston Publishing Co. 1977, 124.

[3] This interview with Bernard Kuhl, in French with Hebrew subtitles, is found at www.lilianeatlan.com and also at YouTube.

[4] The school was named for Gilbert Bloch, a graduate of the elite Ecole Polytechnique and an officer in the Jewish Resistance, murdered by the Wehrmacht on August 8, 1944. For more on this fascinating school, see Denise Gamzon, "L'école Gilbert Bloch http://judaisme.sdv.fr/perso/pivert/

gbloch.htm and https://wikionde.com/article/%C3%89cole_Gilbert-Bloch_d%27OOrsay. There is one book dedicated to the subject: Lucien-Gilles Benguigui, *Un lieu où reconstruire: L'école Gilbert Bloch* (1946-1970), Jerusalem: Ed. Elkana, 2009.

[5] All of Atlan's plays are constructed at the limits of narrative, representation, and temporal and spatial continuity. Of special note is *Un Opéra pour Terezin*, an homage to those who died in the model camp built to house musicians, theatre artists, writers and intellectuals, and to deceive the International Red Cross and other relief and humanitarian groups. An all-night spectacle structured on the Passover Seder, it was first performed in 1997, out-of-doors in Atlan's childhood neighborhood in Montpellier and simultaneously broadcast over France Culture (the national radio station that would air thirteen of her texts). In 1994, the Festival d'Avignon honored the playwright with a retrospective. Under the auspices of Beit Theresienstadt, the French Embassy and French Cultural Services in Israel, a condensed version of *Un Opéra pour Terezin* had a synchronous virtual staged reading on January 27, 2020, with libretti in French, Hebrew, and English, and separate artistic/musical/production teams. See: https://bterezin.org.il/opera/.

[6] Originally published as *Monsieur Fugue, ou le mal de terre*, Paris : Editions du Seuil, 1967. My English translation appears in *Theatre Pieces*, op. cit., which included *The Messiahs* and *The Carriage of Flames and Voices*; and in *Plays of the Holocaust: An International Anthology*, Elinor Fuchs, ed., New York: Theater Communications Group, 1987.

[7] Alejandra Pizarnik (1936-1972), born in Argentina to Ukrainian-Jewish parents; her extensive body of work has been beautifully translated into English by Yvette Siegert; Clarice Lispector (1920-1977), born in Brazil to Ukrainian-Jewish parents, lived most of her life in Recife, capital of Bahía Blanca; her major English translators are Alison Entrekin, Katrina Dodson, Magdalena Edwards, Benjamin Moser, Gregory Rabassa; Vénus Khoury-Ghata (1937-), translated by the eminent American poet Marilyn Hacker.

Prose

FROM

PETITES BIBLES POUR LES MAUVAIS TEMPS
SMALL BIBLES FOR BAD TIMES

Published in Paris in 2001, this book came to fruition in a series of fits and starts that stretched back to the early 1970s. Intensely personal, composed in a mix of genres, *Small Bibles* is structured in four sections, or "canticles," in Bettina Knapp's apt descriptor for a text that relies on themes and variations, verbal harmonics, descants, and dissonance. Atlan writes of her childhood, the war years, the theatre as a way of "killing death." The final section (not included here) is a radio play — a *children's* radio program (surely inspired, in part, by Janush Korzcak), with kids speaking French, Hebrew and Arabic, from Glasgow, Kfar Saba and Kalkiya, their respective languages instantaneously translated, as though by magic, or by a universe that has learned to abet mutual understanding.

In selecting passages for the following excerpt, I wanted the prose to offer a biographical touchstone for Atlan's poetry. Events and crises, persons, places and textual allusions recur in Atlan's oeuvre; I hoped to show the ways in which her poetry, prose, and drama interact. The excerpts are drawn from Liliane's family life, her years of study, her friends and their engagement in publishing a pioneering Jewish journal (*Targum*), and working on street theater in Israel with an international group of Arabs and Jews. More than 35 people appear in this text, and they come bearing names such as God's Not Doing His Job, I'm Replacing Him (Liliane's father), I Will Discover the Secret of Life (Liliane's husband), I Talk to Myself But I'm Still in My Right Mind (nanny to Liliane and her sisters).

While these names are wryly comic in caricaturing family and friends, as well as the author herself, they are not satiric; the narrator refers to her intimates with these tags as an expression of deep empathy and affection. Over the course of the pages to come, some of these names will be abbreviated, as they are in Atlan's French text.

But I'll Get Out Of This: the narrator's family surname
No, But I'll Get Out Of This: the name the narrator gives herself (sometimes referred to or addressed simply as No)
Me, I See It All: the family maid.
I'm Dying: the narrator's mother (based on Madame Elie Cohen)
God's Not Doing His Job, I'm Replacing Him: the narrator's father, based on Elie Cohen
Yes: one of the narrator's sisters
YesNo: one of the narrator's sisters
NoNo: one of the narrator's sisters
YesYes: one of the narrator's sisters
Madame But I'll Get Out of This, aka, Make Me a Price: the narrator's paternal grandmother
No Man Need Apply: the family cook
I Talk to Myself, But I'm Still in My Right Mind: the sisters' nanny (sometimes referred to simply as I Talk to Myself)
I Will Discover the Secret of Life: the narrator's husband Henri Atlan, a young medical student when we meet him; sometimes called simply I Will Discover
Me, I'm Not Getting Married: a close friend of the narrator
Little I Will Discover the Secret of Life: the narrator's daughter (sometimes called Little I Will Discover)
I'm Not Called No Anymore: the narrator reattached to life, as a new mother

I Know Everything and I'm Unhappy: spiritual leader of *I Study*

I Believe in Fairy Tales, I'm Fighting to Make Them Come True: founder of *I Study* (based on Robert Gamzon, Resistance hero and co-founder of the Gilbert Bloch school)

Little God's Not Doing His Job: one of the narrator's sisters

I Was Not Born For Myself: a name the narrator gives herself toward the end of these excerpts

Friends of the Narrator
    I Appear Lighthearted
    I Will Get My Degree Whatever the Cost
    I Talk A Lot and Am Very Charming
    I Will Give Birth to the Messiah
    I Heed My Desire

Polish Students at *I Study*, Collaborators on *Targum*
    I Got Through the War Holding the Hand of My Mother Who Went Insane
    I Was Torn Away From Myself
    Sick for Life

Narrator's friends in Israel
    If You Only Knew How Cold This World Is (sometimes called **If You Only Knew**)
    I Don't Want to Live in an Apartment
    This Country Is Making Me Sick
    Yvonne
    Rami
    Georges
    Ali

IN A RICH HOUSE, IN MARSEILLE, at the end of a war, a young girl is letting herself starve to death.
She is fourteen years old, or fifteen.
Her first name is No; But I'll Get Out of This is her family name.

She goes to school, she studies furiously, she takes long frantic walks on the rocky coast, but she hasn't eaten for months, you can see her bones, she's beginning to lose her memory.

Meals are torture for the entire family.
The maid, Me, I See It All, has a wooden leg, never wears underpants and flaunts it, passes the plates. The mother, I'm Dying, the father, God's Not Doing His Job, I'm Replacing Him, the four sisters, Yes, YesNo, NoNo, YesYes, pretend not to notice when No serves herself.
No puts two or three little bits of something on her plate. She cuts and cuts them again into hundreds of tiny pieces.
She doesn't taste a thing.

Everyone focuses on their own plate, on their fork, on the piece of meat or potato they're about to put in their mouth, everyone acts as if No didn't exist, but everyone watches No and suffers.
No also suffers, from the suffering of her father, of her sisters, of her mother. She would eat to keep them from suffering, if she could.

"Oh please!" I'm Dying cries out, then restrains herself, at the look from God's Not Doing His Job — they'd decided to try keeping quiet, on the advice from Doctor My Practice Is Thriving.

"But how can you deprive yourself of eating," cries the grandmother, Make Me A Price (implication: it's my due. Because I, I'm Madame But I'll Get Out of This, from the High Street, in Montpelier). She made the trip, she made the sacrifice of closing her store in order to help God's Not Doing His Job, I'm Replacing Him make No begin to eat.

"It is so good to eat," God's Not Doing His Job, I'm Replacing Him can't help himself from pleading.

No Man Need Apply, the family cook, comes into the dining room to lend a strong hand:
"My little No, you who are so intelligent, you above all should understand: a motor needs fuel. I made you something special — nana's little turd cakes, 'cause our little No loves chocolate."
The only one who said nothing during the whole meal is I Talk to Myself, but I'm Still in My Right Mind, the nurse for little YesNo, NoNo, YesYes. She watches for the moment when No gets ready to leave for lycée, she waits for her at the door, holding out a tiny piece of buttered bread. No wants to please her. But she can't. I Talk to Myself says nothing, she has tears in her eyes, she stays a moment on the doorstep with her tiny piece of buttered bread, hoping No will turn back and take it.
After school, No buys some chocolate, she eats it on the run so that no one will see, so that this doesn't exist.

By the light of time, and no longer young, No suddenly understands that I Talk to Myself had the gift of intelligence in her love.

I Talk to Myself will in a few days turn eighty-five. She's still in her right mind, and she knows how to enjoy life, even though she lives alone. With the little money she has left, No arranges by telex to send her some flowers.

Flowers to tell you — without words, and after much too long — "Thank you."

[…]

I'm twenty years old, I watch, at the window, for my husband's return, I'm hungry, at the hospital they don't see time passing, the other day the attending physician stuck a nail so deeply into his patient's thigh that he couldn't detach him from the operating table, I Will Discover the Secret of Life choked with laughter as he told me, Ah! That's how it is!

The day after our marriage, I was still stretched out on our bed, he was standing, like the first man on the world's first day, I looked at him, amazed, a man, so that's what a man is! Nothing but that!

Evenings he stuffs his head with the innumerable diseases he'll be tested on during Exams, I accompany Zarathustra in his dance above the abyss, I abandon him in order to write a poem, suddenly I Will Discover the Secret of Life throws himself down on me, I continue my poem in my head, ready to leap up and write, as soon as it's over.

Our apartment is in the heart of the Latin Quarter, and serves as a kind of home for ex-students of our School, I Study, they come when they want, whether or not they're our friends. One evening, I Will Discover takes refuge on the sofa, plunges into a book, gritting his teeth while I try my best to converse with two exceptionally boring visitors. Finally, they leave! He, contemptuous: How can you spend the evening talking such nonsense?

I am at the Faculté des Sciences to register in Chemistry, a discipline apparently deemed necessary for a future philosopher, the corridor twists, I've eaten twelve sardines, sardines won't kill you, but twelve! I'm going to fall, faint, I don't know how I get myself home. I Will Discover:

You're going to have a baby. Me: How dare you laugh! Him: It's not a disaster! Me: I don't want children! I want to write! I told you! Him: Do you want us to prevent this birth? Me: No.

I had the good fortune to pursue my degree under the direction of Gaston Bachelard.[1] I read and re-read his books, on fire, air, earth, water. They teach me to distinguish which metaphors are real and which are false. Those that are true plunge their roots into the living matter of the elements.

At the source of every system, I thought, there is, I was sure of it, a part that was arbitrary, involuntary, inevitable, creative. Perhaps it emanated from a kind of memory of the original abyss engraved in human matter. I dream of writing a poem that would let us understand the feelings imprisoned in matter, be they human or stellar.

That evening, I don't know why, I Will Discover and I felt carefree, we went out strolling in our Rue de Seine, I fall. Oh my God, the child! We go immediately to the hospital where my husband is a resident, they examine me, that child I'd preferred not to think about, I want it to live. The nurses reassure me: Your arm is broken but the baby is fine. I forgive them for being so sensitive to the beauty of the baby's father.

Reading [Bachelard's] *Water and Dreams* plunges me into something luminous, which resists transmission. If my child is a girl, when she herself is expecting a child, she will have access to this luminosity. Evenings, her father studies, out loud, childbirth and its complications, I haven't finished dying of one before he inflicts another, I spend the evenings dying, that's all I do. Except to dream of one day writing a book constructed of the questions he strews about everywhere: Someone is suffering. From what? You investigate by starting with the symptoms. Most symptoms recur in the majority of diseases. They're like identical paths in certain forests, you don't know where to turn, you're lost in the jungle of what you think you know while death does its work in your patient, so go on, dare, do something, anything, but with all your heart!

[. . .]

It's Shabbat, for once we're home alone. Suddenly the child signals that it's preparing to be born. We could go right away to the hospital but I prefer to wait until nightfall, we observe the commandments, we marry our actions with our convictions which are impregnated with the great texts in which fire and mountains speak, birth pangs begin, night falls, we leave, in a hurry. As soon as my daughter opens her eyes, her name announces itself: Little I Will Discover the Secret of Life. The eyes of this child shine with wisdom. I write her a poem, her father goes into ecstasies over the placenta, Little I Will Discover, aged one hour or two, isn't suffering yet on account of her parents.

Me, I'm Not Getting Married pays me a visit, Rue de Seine. I introduce my daughter: Look at her eyes! They're full of wisdom! She: I'm Not Called No Anymore, don't you know that a baby that's three weeks old sees nothing? We're born blind! She tells me about a class with I Know Everything and I'm Unhappy. Me: But in her eyes, her soul. . . . She: "My dear, you got married, became a mother, that's no reason to become stupid."

My daughter sleeps in her carriage in the shade of one of the trees in the Jardin du Luxembourg, across from the statue of Verlaine where the birds arrange to meet. I write my first novel. I blacken hundreds of pages in order not to say that one day I found myself in a mental ward because I was revolted by the horror of so-called humans.

Le Petit Suisse is the café where we liked to meet during the week, after lunch, with our friends from *I Study*: I Appear Lighthearted; I Will Get

My Degree Whatever the Cost; I Talk a Lot and Am Very Charming; Me, I'm Not Getting Married, etc. My father gave us a racing car from the beginning of the century, a Hamilcar, blue, battered, we all pile in, there's a hole in the floor. I Appear Lighthearted pretends to run in the car, so as not to fall out, we cruise through the Latin Quarter, laughing and joking, having a ball. Friday evenings, I Talk a Lot and Am Very Charming often came to see us with his new fiancée, I Will Get My Degree Whatever the Cost. She took the place of my "sister," No, From Rabat. Ever since she was abandoned, ever since she finished her degree, No, From Rabat has been sleeping. She sleeps so as not to kill herself.

I Will Give Birth to the Messiah comes often to see me. I am the only one who knows her secret. If we hadn't been seated at the back of the same class at the lycée in Versailles during the time she doubted there was a God, or if the courses taught by I Know Everything and I'm Unhappy hadn't given me the keys, I would never have brought her into this domain of light and fire, which resembles the Garden of Knowledge.

My father wanted to give us a luxurious car. We didn't want this. He insisted. We: If you really want to do something nice for us, give us the means to create our own magazine. We dream of translating the key ideas of the Hebraic tradition into the language of western civilization. Our idea captivates him. The Editorial Board comes together of itself: I Will Discover the Secret of Life; I Talk a Lot and Am Very Charming; I Will Get My Degree Whatever the Cost; I'm No Longer Named No; Me, I'm Not Getting Married, who protests: Our magazine won't work without I Know Everything. I Talk a Lot, with his habitual charm: We Know. He doesn't have time to come to Le Petit Suisse, but we won't do anything without him.

Our meetings happen spontaneously, wherever we find ourselves, most often in our living room, Rue de Seine. We search for a name for our

Review. One day, I Will Discover finds it: *Targum*.[2] I Talk A Lot: Brilliant! The girlfriends: What does it mean? I Talk A Lot: Translation. When they returned from Babylon the Hebrews no longer understood their own language, it was necessary to translate the Torah into Aramean. Today, it's the meaning of our texts that needs to be translated. I Will Discover: we'll put that on every cover. You'll be Editor in Chief. I Talk a Lot: And you'll be Publication Director. I Will Discover: But I know nothing! I Talk a Lot: Same here!

The first issue of *Targum* is ready. The cover will be black. The word *Targum*, written in blue, crossed with its double written in ivory white, will occupy the center of a geometric figure flanked by two stars. At the top and bottom of the cover, these words, from a poem by Jocelyn Askénazi-Gerson[3]:

Even if the voice is silenced . . .
. . . the echo does not fade

Here comes my father, in his arms a sumptuous toy for his grand-daughter. He likes the first issue of *Targum*, he admires the poem on the opening page. The article by his son-in-law, "The Role of the Inhuman," both fascinates and troubles him:

Why do you say that the fate of our people is inhuman?
I Will Discover: Because the point of its existence is to show how to transcend what we are. The true destiny of man is to become superhuman.
God Does His Work Badly: Me, I like us just as we are!
His Daughter: We do need a handful of men to demonstrate that something else is possible, that another, more human way, of being men will someday be possible.
God Does His Work Badly: My children, I do not agree with the way

you think! Why am I so proud and happy to help you spread such ideas?

He bursts out laughing then, suddenly turns sad.

I had to quit school very young in order to make money, I studied Law on my own, in the train when I traveled up North to visit factory owners, I was barely nineteen, I wore a bowler hat to impress them, all on my own I discovered Hugo, Valéry, then later, Fleg . . .

Of his nostalgia for study, he was never cured.

The first issue of *Targum* is out, we discuss it, passionately. Our readers: It's great, but why do you write in a such an obscurant style? Us: Have you ever spent time with us without talking about *Being and Nothingness*?[4] Them: Still! People are saying they can't read you without a bottle of aspirin in reach! And that poem: "I sawed through the golden sky with the force of an idea!" And sub-titles and subheads like: "Dereliction of Thought!" I Appear Lighthearted: Still, it's great! His only argument being his charming smile.

At *I Study*, in the Sukkah,[5] under the stars, surrounded by ancient trees, we listen to I Know Everything and I'm Unhappy dream of our people's metamorphosis: It will happen through the re-establishment of the truth contained in our Texts, which for too long has been hidden, denatured. Even before we were exterminated, we were sick with the most dangerous of famines, that of the mind. A starving mind destroys, nourishes death. Killing death is a delicate matter. It must be done wisely, at the right moment. We will have to dare to break with the teachers we have now. They're passing on the errors that they were taught. How to make them understand without injuring them? I've barely begun and I already have so many enemies! He describes his enemies, with such humor that we burst out laughing, we feel privileged to be his confidants. Me, I'm Not Getting Married can't hide the passionate love she feels for her Teacher, who is married, with two children.

Targum appears regularly. We are very proud of it. Friends flood into our home, to discuss the enigmas of the world, we like finding connections between myths and the sages, descriptions of the birth of the universe are enthralling and uncertain, our abstract language gives us the impression that we know how to think, he who is hungry shall eat, if I want to have a bit of food left for my daughter I need to hide it. Gi'me! Gi' me! she says over and over, I finally understand what she wants: she wants me to look at her.

Jewish students who were ferociously secular but fascinated by I Know Everything sometimes came to *I Study*. Among them were: I Got Through the War Holding the Hand of My Mother Who Went Insane; I Was Torn Away From Myself; and Sick for Life. They'd fled Poland. Their families were dead. They're bound to each other by deep friendship. We give them a platform in *Targum*.

Sick for Life doesn't write. He can't. He hates his native language, which is Polish. He loves no other language. He haunts writers, well-known and not, exhorting them to re-write the last chapter of the Bible, the Extermination. One day, in the street, trembling with a somber joy, he tells me that Rudniki has done it: It's called *The Golden Windows*.[6] Read it, right away. It's brilliant. He gives me a full account. But it's inadequate. So, he, Sick for Life, starts again.

I am at the Bibliothèque Nationale, I watch the people who are reading all around me. By the light of that which is no more, I recognize the aura of one person: the man with the black carry bag. He orders books, he doesn't read them, he doesn't do anything. He speaks to no one. His bag is dirty, worn, maybe there's nothing inside but he keeps it close, it's all he has. His gaze is far off, as though he's can see through walls. What he sees is no more. His mourning is silent. Absolute.

During the war, *I Believe in Fairly Tales, I'm Fighting to Make Them Come True*, created a network of Jewish resistance. They made their base at a farm, in Lautrec, which he'd gotten from the Vichy government by employing the return-to-the-earth mystique. I want to tell his story. My book will be called *The Little Star Bearers*, the yellow star, of course, but also an inner, unsuspected star, revivified and radiant with their life force and shared struggle.

In order to write this novel, I go visit the people who lived the story. She who survives in my memory is a young woman who was raising her two children alone. She was in charge of an orphanage for girls whose parents had been deported and never returned. Her husband, a young rabbi who dreamed of recovering the perfume of study, had been murdered by the Nazis before the birth of their second daughter. She, Marguerite, couldn't do everything all alone. There she was, barely able to live, but happy for the sake of the orphans, a group that included her daughters.

One day, in Jerusalem, I go see Rachel Kohn. She was the wife of Léo Kohn. They'd come from Germany. They were refugees with their daughter in Lautrec. Shabbat, on the farm, Léo, nourished with the wisdom of the Hasidim, sang, those who understood him recount that he gave them desire, pride, and happiness in being Jews. He wanted to go to Palestine by way of Spain, having first to cross the Pyrenees, and that's where he was murdered. Rachel received me at home, she'd married Léo's brother, given him a daughter. She is very calm, very beautiful. She offers me a frugal meal served with such refinement that it felt princely. I don't ask any questions, I can see that she loves Léo, it emanates from her whole being, her brother-in-law and husband accepts this, respects it, as does she. One day, a long time later, I see her from a distance, coming out of a concert hall, buffeted by the wind, by age, she's so frail, a shadow, unforgettable.

I didn't know Gilbert Bloch, but I had the privilege of reading his journal. He wrote while holding a notebook across his lap, in a remote spot at the farm in Lautrec. He'd asked I Believe in Fairy Tales to allow him the right to isolate himself, even if for only fifteen minutes a day. He had a visceral need for solitude. He'd studied at the Polytechnique, was at heart a Christian. Constrained to re-become Jewish, he suffered from not knowing what it meant to be a Jew. From that dilemma arose his dream of a Jewish polytechnical school where one would study, at the highest level, the modern sciences, Jewish tradition, and ancient wisdoms from all over the world. I only knew him from his photo, which reigned in the common room of *I Study*, and from his dream: to create the future through study and wisdom.

I Believe in Fairy Tales is in Paris for a few days. He comes to see us. He tells about the life of the gar'hín, the little group from *I Study* that left to live in Israel, first at Sdé-Eliahu, a religious kibbutz lower than sea-level, where they're doing the apprenticeships to prepare them to create their own model-kibbutz in which the secular and religious will live together in harmony. It's possible, crucial, or our people will have no future either on earth or in its Book. I tell him about *The Little Star Bearers*, I ask him questions about life at Lautrec. He tells me, with an inexhaustible pleasure, about the loves born in that farm, and which became, for him included, legendary.

The new issue of *Targum* keeps being delayed. I Know Everything and Am Unhappy doesn't have time to write his article. Sometimes he comes to complain how such-and-such and so-and-so won't leave him alone until he tells them the exact moment they can resume frolicking after observing the laws of family purity. A little girl is born before her parents are wed. In our little world of respect for the Law, it's a crime. I'm charged with finding a nurse for this baby. Born too soon, as was my mother, she will long bear the imprint of the sadness surrounding her birth. I passionately respect the 613 commandments handed down at Sinai, but still, in the name of what, can the birth of a child conceived in love be a crime?

One day an Orthodox commando comes for coffee, as soon as they leave, I open the windows wide.

[. . .]

Finally, the seventh issue of *Targum* is published. Feeling old, I re-read it, and see that our articles were linked to each other like the instruments played by musicians in a single orchestra. There was nothing by I Know Everything and I Am Unhappy. He never stopped promising a text for the following month, and, in the end, we had to move on, we wanted the magazine to appear.

I Know Everything and I Am Unhappy, shortly before dying: You wanted to liberate yourselves from me.

Me: From your history. A history of exceptional love, deliriously, inhumanly pure, given to young people, innovators perhaps, by virtue of their ideas, but they couldn't, in their own lives, liberate themselves from their principles. We didn't yet know to what degree this lack of intelligence — real intelligence, that which comes from the heart — would destroy us.

[. . .]

We'd left the Rue de Seine to go live in the country, near a river, with the company of trees, of birds. Of course, my husband loves this hermitage, he needs all this green when he returns from the operating room, but me, trees! I need to be surrounded by living people, to go into bookshops, browse through books, stroll up and down the boulevard . . .

One day, at *I Study*, we were by chance seated across from one another, we who were always so talkative looked at each other for a long time, in silence, trembling.

My son had just been born. If he were already able to speak, he would say: My mother doesn't even notice that I was born! No, I do, but your grandfather died just after your birth, you look so much like him, I don't dare take you in my arms, I look at you, with love, a silent love that can't be separated from mourning.

[. . .]

One day, at *I Study*, I'm sitting on the threshold, absent, suddenly my whole body is shaken by a brutal slap. I Will Discover had struck me: Your father is dead. You went with him. Now, you must come back to us. In his eyes, in his voice, such sadness, such tenderness. I get up. I go rejoin my children.

I Know Everything and I Am Unhappy introduces I Will Discover the Secret of Life to the Kabbala.[7] I Will Discover will be his disciple, he alone among the former students of *I Study* will do. When he returns to the Hermitage, he tells me how worlds are created, and I see nothing except the pleasure he takes in putting an abstract name on imaginary circles. If I weren't a woman, I'd have received this teaching directly from I Know Everything, who was still alive then. I Know Everything had the gift of metaphor. It's through metaphor that thought lives in the heart. If wisdom doesn't come from the heart, what can it illuminate?

We get our kosher meat by mail, we live too far from the rue des Rosiers to go shopping for it. I have to salt it, rinse it, without using a plate or knife reserved for dairy, otherwise, it's the river: I Will Discover adores dunking the plates that I have rendered impure. He murmurs the appropriate blessing, with a note of amusement. Of course, he doesn't believe in the need to do all this. So, why do you do it? Out of respect for the Law. We need a Law. On the Eve of Shabbat, I have to put a casserole on a casserole on a casserole so that the plates will warm each other not by fire but from the steam of the steam of the first of the steams. The result:

the broth I give my son is cold. What good is it to study the secret of the creation of worlds if, in the end, you give your child cold soup? We need a Law, you say over and over, but why this one? Because it's so harsh? You who study the secret of worlds, including your own, do you know why?

[. . .]

Here I am in the narrow little streets of the Old City of Jerusalem, letting myself be pulled along in the flow of pedestrians, we're going to see the Wall[8] for the first time. In the square that hasn't yet been renovated, the form of the houses, the color of the stones, the expression of a face, the flight of a bird, its fleeting shadow on a bit of wall, everything excites and bewilders me, I'm hungry, I want to leave, but the light has just changed, illuminating this bit of stone, this face, differently. After several long hours, an Israeli soldier asks me: But, finally, what do you see? How could I tell him? Most often, it's something small, revealed by the light. The light here reveals what it shines upon. The light of the Messiah, say the religious. No. The light of the desert. I feel the presence of all those whose shadows the desert holds.

I climb up toward the Esplanade and there, before the Mosque, I feel defeated, humiliated, Palestinian. I check into a room in the Hotel Petra, an Arab hotel at the entrance to the Old City. The owner and his employees are listening, with such passion, to the hateful radio of their brothers. At night I hear screaming, I think it's coming from the prison across from the hotel: it's cats, in their season of love. I go, I come, unable to understand the words, I listen to the voices. Arrogance hides fear, courtesy hides hatred, and sometimes, above it all, what dominates is the pleasure of talking to each other, of doing business, of being alive. What if I improvised, right here, on these steps, a theatre piece in which I recounted the long, drawn-out death of my people, despised because they bore witness, involuntarily, to eternal and infinite human ugliness. You would pity us, you who have become our victims. So, healed of not being loved, we could win your trust, return your lands, your houses, your dignity. An impossible dream, but by living side by side, connections could be made, sometimes even marriages. I write to Kateb Yacine,[9] I know he's no fanatic, I propose that together we write our tragedy, he from the Arab side, I from the Jewish side, in this way we will die, but in theatres, not in real life. He replies: You are my sister in poetry. We'll meet at my place, in Paris. Him: Lyricism is no longer possible. We need to find the tone for farce. That's how horrible we are. Another day, on the telephone: If I tell the truth, they will kill me.

[...]

In order to write a play with Kateb Yacine, I've dragged my family to Israel. This country can be defined in two words: sunflower seeds. I've never seen so much chewing of sunflower seeds and with such nonchalance, such violence, so much art in the expression of all the nuances of feeling in the mere act of spitting out what's left of the shells, on the terraces of cafés, in the streets, in living rooms. The highest praise is reserved for never hitting one's neighbors! The savants of the Weizmann Institute are famous for their intelligence, but is it known that they also excel in the art of spitting sunflower seeds? If the prophets rose from their graves and saw them, their rage would make the earth tremble. Though who knows? Maybe they too were sunflower-seed virtuosi! Kateb has just sent me a postcard, from Moscow. I answer in my head: We could call our farce: *The War of the Sunflower Soldiers*!! Let the world tremble! In the Art of the Sunflower Seed everyone is more gifted than the other.

One day, I'm resting in my garden, the neighbor's son returns from Gaza where he's doing his military service. He recounts with what pleasure he'd beaten up an Arab who was trying to climb into a bus. I don't express myself well enough in Hebrew to tell him what I think.

[. . .]

So that I can write in peace, I've been given the key to one of the antinuclear shelters at the Weizmann Institute.[10] I open the lead door, I walk past the decontamination showers, I go down into the earth. Hypnotized, I look at the black walls, the benches, the stored-up limestone: in case of an atomic accident the savants keep pursuing their work. One day, I've Lost My Bearings comes to visit me. He's in ecstasies at the Mount of Olives. . . . The sun sets, the beauty of the Mount of Olives turns supernatural.

[. . .]

I'm back in Rehovot. I feel like I've fallen into the void. Your analyses are normal, the doctor declares. Me, I silently look back at him: Here, when the doctors go on strike, fewer people die. Him: Are you happy? Me, in silence: If I had the courage to divorce, then maybe. But . . .

Out loud: Happy in Rehovot, no, Doctor. I tried Jerusalem, that didn't work either. Him, in silence: My poor lady, if I'd only left this country where, like you, I'm dying! But where to go? Out loud: Take six valiums a day, and come back to see me. Israeli valium sends me down a staircase plunged in a black abyss, the steps are covered with the pieces of bloody beasts, it leads me down a chute without end, even though I wake up. Result: I throw out the valium and make a rule for myself: Never again consult a Zionist physician.

I've met a long-haired researcher and his wife. They're called We Don't Want to Live in an Apartment. They're French. We like getting together to bitch, and to laugh. Along with their friends from the Institute of Agronomy, located across from the Weizmann, they introduce me to some Palestinians. I introduce them to Israeli theatre. One evening, to recover from the play we'd just suffered through, we strolled through a garden in Tel-Aviv. Suddenly, one of us, This Country Is Making Me

Sick, climbs onto a bench and strikes a theatrical pose. I Don't Want to Live in an Apartment shouts: I'm selling this statue! His friend, If You Only Knew How Cold This World Is: You butted in! That statue is mine! This store is mine! Passersby are laughing, clapping. Our vocation is born: we'll make political theatre in the streets of Tel-Aviv.

We prepare our spectacle in my apartment. If You Only Knew How Cold This World Is, the only one among us born in Israel and who speaks a real Hebrew, fills out the scene spontaneously born the other evening: I Don't Want to Live in an Apartment putting This Country Is Making Me Sick up for sale. He shouts: Passersby! Look at this handsome young man exiled from Chile! Whoever buys him will only have to look at him in order to escape being here! I arrive. I shout: The rest, we'll improvise. Everyone: In Hebrew?! Him: You will all be new immigrants, each one with the accent of the country they've fled. Us: That's great! Him: My family comes from Yemen. We have never stopped speaking King Solomon's Hebrew. It's our pride, our only wealth.

In Dizengoff Street the café terraces are full, we walk among the cars, beating pots and pans, shouting: Free Show! 11pm! Dizengoff Street! In the front of the Alcheh Library! A show like no other! Fr-eeee-eee! Fr-eeee-eee! After which we head for the sea. My friends are yelling, I've never been onstage! I'll be a disaster! Our veterinarian: We absolutely have to eat. If You Only Knew How Cold This World Is, as though he were yelling for help: Hummus! We find a table at a cheap little place and wolf down our food. Me, to reassure them: I'm the only professional here. I'm risking everything. You, nothing. Everyone, yelling: It's time! Here we are in the front of the Alcheh Library. Everyone, under their breath: There are people! Me, in French: This is a catastrophe I hadn't foreseen. Out loud, in my Hebrew from the south of France, to the audience: If you'd be so kind, please leave a little space so the actors can put on the show! I Don't Want to Live in an Apartment, gone pale, whispers to me, in French: My secretary is here, she's recognized me. Me, whispering back, in French: Just go on. And he does: This handsome young male exiled from Chile is for sale! He's beautiful as a statue, but he breathes! Someone else: This guy has taken my place! The two of them: I was here first! I'm going to kill you! They fight. One, in his agonies: If you could only respect me! The two, dying while still killing each other: But you took my place! I was before you! I have no place to go! And it all starts again. Our audience steps forward, comes close so they can hear, they're all but smothering us, the show is over, they're not leaving. We talk together, for hours. Finally, our neighbors' real name is pronounced: they're no longer terrorists, but Palestinians.

Shortly after the Yom Kippur War, by chance I cross paths, in Jerusalem, with If You Only Knew How Cold This World Is. Him: I just got back from Sinai. I'm one of only two survivors in my unit. We absolutely have to make theatre with Palestinians. It's the only way for us to talk to each other, to understand each other, to one day make peace. Me: I return to Paris tomorrow! Him: I'm going to get some Israelis and Palestinians together, we'll learn to act, when you come back, we'll be ready. Me: Okay. Work with a professional director. We'll play in the streets. We'll make street theatre.

One day, in Jerusalem, I discovered by chance that Deir Yassine,[11] that Arab village whose inhabitants were massacred by the Jews in 1948, has become a hospital for the incurably mentally ill. Today it's named for King Saul, the king who went mad during the time of the Hebrews, who, tired of being prophets, wanted to become a people among other peoples. This story is but one story among others, but it's the most nerve-shattering, for it embroils the characters in the play I'm writing, in which I'm attempting in my paltry way find a way to envision peace as a possibility.

If You Only Knew How Cold This World Is has assembled Israelis and Palestinians, they've been working together, they're ready. I return to join them. I go visit the director who's been helping them, Joyce Miller.[12] I start talking about the village called Deir-Yassine, a man with a strikingly sad demeanor, her husband, cuts me off: I'm the one who named the place Kfar Shaül because that's where King Saul went mad. He'd become a king like any other king, that's what drove him mad. At the time, I was in charge of the hospital. I'm a psychiatrist.

One day, there's a knock at my door. It's two Palestinians. The older one: We've come to tell you that we can't make theatre with you. They'd put us in quarantine. Me: Would you like some coffee? Them: Yes. I prepare the coffee and carry it in. The older one: Your cups are dirty. Me: I'm so sorry, I'll go wash them. Him: They're still dirty. Me: I'll wash them again.

I bring more coffee and, distressed, I say: They're getting dirtier and dirtier. The older one: Even so, your coffee is good. He swallows, and declares: You're living in an Arab house. Me: No, I'm not! Him, very sad: I'm telling you that you're living in an Arab house. Not one of us speaks. They could throw a bomb out my window and hit Radio Israel. Me: What is your name? The older one: Ali. I'm a theatre director and I work in a garage. Me: And you? The younger one: Samih. I'm an actor in Ali's show and I work with him at the garage.

Everyone wants to kill us: that's the theme that gushes out in Hebrew, Arabic, English, French, Polish, and Swedish, in our first improvisations. Two Palestinian Israelis, Mohammed, a professional actor, and Ibrahim, a pharmacy student, join us. One evening, Ibrahim, who's just been awarded his degree, announces that he cannot practice his profession in suitable conditions because he's Palestinian, he's despairing, he's come to tell us that he won't be back, he gets to his feet to leave with Orna, his

Israeli fiancée. I beg them to stay. I tell him about my own suffering as a Jewish child, and my rebellion, and I say that maybe this helps me to understand him. Everyone tells their own story, so that he too can understand. He's very moved, but even sadder: You are all very nice, but you can't do anything for me. I'd rather go home. Me: It's true, we can't do anything for you, but you'll be less sad with us than all alone in your room. I get up, open my armoire, take out a bunch of clothes, throw them on the floor. Hadassah forms them into a sort of raft, Mohammad joins her, they start rowing, shouting: We're fleeing our country where we haven't the right to love each other, we'll find a land where we can love each other in total freedom, if we find none, then this raft will become our land, our children will be born here, and grow up, and marry — Ibrahim, Orna, don't be alone, come back to us, their cry becomes a chant, and it's so beautiful, there's no more question of Ibrahim leaving us.

My room becomes our rehearsal space. One day, I tell them — and my Hebrew ignites their laughter — that we must absolutely rehearse outside since we're doing our show outside. Where? Ideas start to fuse. Yvonne, joking: The Gardens of the Knesset! Rami: Brilliant! At night no one's there, but it's all lit up. Me: Rehearsal there tomorrow at nightfall. Georges, don't forget your violin. Here we are in the Gardens. Ibrahim becomes a blind entrepreneur brandishing his cane and threatening his employees, in the name of their despair they're building houses on top of those that were already there, without saying a word, Ali turns away, heads down toward the street, his back increasingly bent, rendering tangible, without saying a single word, the despair of refugees. Georges shouts: My violin is wet! Wet! Us: It's not raining! Him: The dew! Dew! We watch him leave for the city, holding his violin in his arms as though it were a child while Ali, in exile two steps away, doesn't yet want to rejoin us.

One evening, Ali and If You Only Knew How Cold the World Is go digging in the ground to prove that it belongs to them. Ali uncovers his grandfather's shoes. If You Only Knew digs up King Saul, who's missing his head. All good, but we need to build a spectacle. I propose that each one come in from a different point in the space shouting in their native language: Everyone wants to kill me! Instead of which, they start fighting, screaming. Ali discreetly suggests that I come tomorrow to the Old City to see how he works with his actors.

The play they're rehearsing is simple: from beginning to end, Israelis slap Palestinians. Ali slaps his actors. They don't protest. He accompanies me as far as the gate to the Old City: Do like me, slap them, as hard as you can, it'll work.

Here we are again in our Gardens. We take it from the beginning. Once again everyone makes their own scene and everyone screams. I don't hit anyone but I do lift them up, one after the other, as though they were sacks, in order to move them to a spot of my own choosing. Stupefied, their acting is not as bad as usual. No less stupefied, I watch them.

In spite of Ali's lesson, I'm not a director, they're not actors, we're going to bring shame on ourselves when we play on the campus of the University of Giv'at-Ram. The date is set: Sunday. This is our last rehearsal. The boys are all late. Finally, they arrive, in a terrible state: The army has called us up. For Sunday! We don't know if we'll be able to be in the play! Me, in silence: May the army take them. Out loud: We'll be on the campus starting at Noon, we'll make everything ready and wait for you.

I go to Giva't-Ram, hoping for a miracle, which is to say, that the army has kept the boys. Alas, they're all there. As well as actors from the seven Palestinian theatres in the Old City. Me: Freaked out, trying not to show it: Where shall we do this? If You Only Knew: Right here, in the middle of campus, they can't not see us! Me: And how will they know we're going to put on a show? If You Only Knew, and Leah: We'll climb on the tables in the cafeteria to announce it! I don't know who among us: Don't forget the tables in the Library! We put on a sorry little show, but the cleaning women of the University discovered that Palestinians exist, professors are delighted that we dared to make theatre together, even though it was bad. Ali invites I Will Discover and me to come see the seven shows that will be playing later in the Old City, including, of course, his own. We don't understand anything, except that they do real theatre.

We don't rehearse anymore but we still get together. Our friendship persists in spite of the attacks in the Jewish city and the searches in the Arab city. In the worst moments, we say nothing, but we stay together.

[. . .]

I Will Discover the Secret to Life and I are leaving the court house. We have just divorced.
He doesn't want to take my hand. Me: Not even to say good-bye? Him: I no longer have the right.

Observation, long afterward: some of my heart's debris may still be stuck to some of your heart's debris. It appears that universes are populated by dead stars. That that's what they're made of. That there isn't anything else. Except, maybe, with time, due to erosion, some metamorphoses.

One day I run into a friend from before, I Will Get My Degree Whatever the Cost. We haven't seen each other for years. She: I divorced, I found my freedom. I listen to my desire. I have learned to listen, to respect, to indulge, my desire. And you? Me: I've had my moments of happiness. Door closed. Concert disrupted.

I move away from the window so I don't throw myself into the void. I have friends whose mothers committed suicide, they never got over it. I haven't given much to my children. But at least, I will save them that. One day when I'm feeling better I write to my daughter, I say how for the sake of her and her brother I managed not to throw myself out the window. After a few months I receive her response: a white shawl she made herself, crocheted herself, for me. I have it still, guard it with my life.

[. . .]

I often have this dream: With a group of tourists, I'm visiting Auschwitz, which is now a museum. Like all tourists we take photos, on the ramp, in the blocks, in the shower rooms, in the gas chamber, suddenly we realize, too late, that the gas is turned on. And that we will never be able to say anything about this hell.

The dream of the denatured name: I'm in a hospital corridor, I'm supposed to be operated on right away, the nurses have forgotten me. My friend, I Heed My Desire, throws herself on me, her desire this evening is to steal the soul of my soul, she tears from me that which renders me alive. Of my name, I Was Not Born for Myself, only Myself remains. Prey. Bird of prey.

How to revive the divine spark buried in the depths of our flesh and our soul? We believe we're revitalized but the famine from which we suffer worsens.

I'm in Jerusalem. I take a few steps on a road from which the Dead Sea is visible. There is the desert and suddenly the beginning of something else. This border, so thin, is the place where light undergoes its metamorphoses. The place that gave rise, perhaps, to the idea that we must confront the supernatural. And everyone, in their language and according to their desire, develops their Fable.

If our passion for bloody and holy wars came from our refusal to take stock of our solitude in the universe. If we could feel the vulnerability of the universe itself. If confronting the abyss rendered all the more precious this fleeting miracle of being alive.

I Know Everything and I'm Unhappy gives his final class. He can hardly breathe. A second cancer has developed in the lung already operated on. He tells us, by the light of the Kabbala, of the infinite solitude that preceded the creation of worlds, that of man and woman, of the murder of brother by brother, the impossible fraternity among brothers since the first days of the world, open a window, he asks, one can't breathe in here, but he's the only one who's struggling, he takes up where he left off, he's so witty that we laugh, laugh to ward off despair. After class everyone wants to talk with him, he gestures for me to come close, he creates a void around us, he needs to express his sorrow . . .

A few days later, he calls me: I'm in the hospital. I wrote a poem last night. Can you come read it to me? He's pale, a machine is helping him breathe, he's still in danger of dying. I read his poem, in Hebrew it's called *There is = Wall*; in French, *Le Mystère du Mur* (*The Mystery of the Wall*). It's a human cri de coeur bound to a cosmic cri de coeur. It's a poem that goes beyond poetry, it's a teaching that gives new life to teaching. Me: You revitalize the Kabbala. He insists I make sure there's no betrayal of that which must remain hidden. We suppress two or three words.

[. . .]

One day, in Jerusalem, while I was doing some research on the Jews of Salonika [where Liliane's family originated], I was sent to an historian who, instead of answering my questions, asked why I was interested. "I'm one of them." I talk about my father, of all the people who saved us during the war because they loved my father. He writes down everything, to my surprise. I want to give them the Medal of the Righteous Among Nations![13] They're all dead! So what? We'll give it to their children! Monsieur So-and-So didn't have any! So what! What's his address? I'm telling you he's been dead forty years! If you really want to give the Medal of the Righteous to a truly just person, give it to I Talk to Myself but I'm in My Right Mind! Who's that? The nurse who took care of my little sisters. She risked her life to take care of us during the war. A long time after, I asked her why she'd done it. Your father was so good that God couldn't allow anyone to touch his children. Write a few lines about her, she'll have her Medal. When? She's already ninety-five years old! The directors of the Department of the Just are volunteers, they don't meet every day. What if she dies? We'll give it to her children. She didn't have any, she never married! I'll write the paper immediately and you give her the Medal this year.

She received her Medal at her rest home, a few months before she died. My sister, Little God's Not Doing His Job, loved her and went often to see her. She'd arranged the ceremony with the refined and luxurious taste that made her a star in her profession, with that elegance of heart that made her unique.

An ambassador from Israel attended. I Talk to Myself has trouble sitting down and difficulty walking, she has become truly very old. When she smiles she is marvelous. She strikes a chord with the ambassador who tells her that he too had to hide during the war, he's just given the Medal of Yad Vashem to the person who saved him.

Here we are in the dining room of the rest home. The pensioners are waiting for us, astounded that their elder who makes so little noise, who takes up so little space, is receiving such honors. I Talk to Myself is so proud of her Medal that she weeps.

Little God's Not Doing and I accompany her to her room, she shows us her Medal all over again, she's as happy as a child. Without vanity. "A saint, you are a saint!" Little God tells her. How will you manage when you no longer have the strength to go downstairs to the dining room?"

She goes out to see the woman Director. We're alone. I remember that one day, when I was little, she'd let me understand that once upon a time she'd been in love. Again I ask her the question—why did she do it. She tries to remember. No, she says. And with that marvelous smile that she's had since becoming so old, she tells me: "Because they were children."

That was her true name: Because They Were Children.

Notes

[1] **Gaston Bachelard (1884-1962)**, French philosopher perhaps best known for *The Poetics of Space*, was a major influence on Foucault, Althusser, Derrida, and Bourdieu, among others. Atlan studied under Bachelard at the Sorbonne; the book she refers to here is *L'eau et les rêves*, originally published in 1942; translated, by Edith Farrell, as *Water and Dreams: An Essay on the Imagination of Matter*, and published by The Pegasus Foundation (The Bachelard Translations), 1983.

[2] ***Targum***, the name of the journal published by Atlan and her friends at *I Study*, refers to spoken Aramaic translations of Jewish scripture, for audiences whose languages were not Hebrew. The practice goes back to the period of the Second Temple, 516 BCE-70 CE.

[3] **Jocelyn Askénazi-Gerson**, French philosopher and poet who also published a study of Hebrew grammar to shed light on the work of Spinoza.

[4] ***Being and Nothingness: An Essay on Phenomenological Ontology,*** Jean-Paul Sartre's touchstone text on existentialism, originally published in 1943, it came out in English in 1956.

[5] **Sukkah**, the temporary dwellings made by Jews for the week-long holiday of Sukkot, which celebrates the harvest and God's protection of the Jews on their way out of Egypt. Families and communities cover these dwellings, in which they take their meals, with foliage, and often decorate with fruits, cornucopia, and colored lights.

[6] *The Golden Windows,* a 1963 novel by Adolf Rudnicki (1912-1990), a leading writer of the "Jewish school" in postwar Polish literature. Other major works include the short-story collection, *Epoch of the Ovens, The Merchant of Lodz,* and volumes of autobiography. Captured by the invading Nazis in 1939, he managed to escape, participate in the Warsaw Uprising, and aid fellow Jews. Born into a Hasidic family, he wrote texts that resonated with ancient teachings, and experimented with blending styles, genres, and mediums (such as expressionism). https://yivoencyclopedia.org/article.aspx/Rudnicki_Adolf

[7] **Kabbala**, ancient mystical tradition of interpreting Jewish canonical texts.

[8] **The Wall,** known in Hebrew as the Kotel, this is the holiest site in Judaism. It is a limestone remnant of the Western Wall of the Second Temple, a place of worship from 516BCE until 70CE, when it was destroyed by the Romans. Built to replace Solomon's Temple, which had been destroyed by Nebuchadnezzar in 585BCE, it is also sometimes referred to as The Wailing Wall, since under centuries of Christian rule (368-638), Jews were only allowed on the Temple Mount on Tisha 'b'Av, a liturgical day of mourning to commemorate this history of temple destructions. In Islam, the site is referred to Al Buraq, after the steed on which the Prophet Mohammad was ascended into heaven. The Al-Aqsa mosque is on the Eastern border of the temple complex. Under the British Mandate Palestine (1920-1948), Moslems had full ownership of the Wall complex, but Jews were allowed access on certain days of worship. From 1948-1967, Jews were prohibited from the site by Jordanian control;

after winning the Six-Day War, Israel regained control of the Old City and created the Esplanade around the Temple Mount, as well as a Jewish residential and commercial neighborhood. Liliane first visited this site very soon after the end of the Six-Day War and, as the passage demonstrates, her reactions were complicated: she was suffused with feelings of numinous Jewish homecoming, as well as shame and mourning for the Arabs whose homes had been destroyed as part of the new Israeli construction.

[9] **Kateb Yacine (1962-1989)**, an Algerian Berber playwright and novelist, who was active in anti-colonialist politics, for which he spent time in Algerian jails. Having settled in France, he declared, "I write in French to tell the French that I am not French." Although he also wrote in Algerian Arabic, he considered French "the Algerians' spoil of war." He was controversial in Algeria for his loyalty to Berber traditions and language (supervising translations of his work into Tamazight), for his belief in gender equality, and for opposing the requirement that women wear a headscarf. He was active with the public intellectuals of his time, including with Sartre and Brecht. Yacine's plays were performed at the Festival d'Avignon and throughout Europe; *Mohammad, Get Your Suitcase*, about the Algerian migration to France, is one of his landmark plays. For his 1986 play about Nelson Mandela he was awarded France's Grand Prix National des Lettres. A leader in popular political theatre and street performance, he was a friend and tutelary influence on Liliane Atlan. One of his novels, *Nedja*, was translated by Richard Howard and published, in 1991, by the University Press of Virginia.

[10] **Weizmann Institute of Science,** founded in 1934, in the city Rehovot, is an elite multi-disciplinary institution offering graduate, post-doctoral, and cutting-edge research in mathematics, physics, chemistry, biochemistry, biology, and in innovative cross-disciplinary fields. One of the first electronic computers was built here in 1954-55.

[11] **Deir Yassin**, an Arab Muslim village near Jerusalem with a population, in 1948, of about 600. Having signed a peace agreement with the nearby Orthodox Jewish community of Givat Shaul, it was prosperous and stable, until skir-

mishes between Jewish and Arab militias broke out in neighboring towns, and Deir Yassin came under pressure from both sides. On April 9, 1948, extremist right-wing Jewish paramilitary forces (the Haganah and the Stern Gang faction of the Irgun) attacked Deir Yassin, killing hundreds of men, women, and children in a vicious massacre. Jews from Givat Shaul attempted to thwart the attackers and aid their neighbors; immediately after the massacre, the Jewish Agency wrote a letter of apology to Jordan's King Abdullah. Right-wing nationalists claimed the battle a victory and an important signal that Israel would be undaunted in its fight for Jerusalem (which it would recapture in 1967). In 1949, in the face of protest (and political pressure from eminent Jewish scholars and theologians, including Martin Buber) the Israeli government began building on the ruins of Deir Yassin the Jerusalem neighborhood of Givat Shaul Bet. The Kfar Shaul Mental Health Center was built in 1951, and incorporated some of Deir Yassin's abandoned and partly destroyed houses and buildings. That Deir Yassin was turned into a Jewish mental hospital has been used — by Liliane and others — as a metaphor for the insanity of the Arab-Israeli conflict. https://www.google.com/search?q=deir+yassin+wikipedia&oq=Deir+Yassin+wiki&aqs=chrome.0.0j69i57j0l2.3764j1j8&sourceid=chrome&ie=UTF-8.

[12] **Joyce Miller** (1919-2009) founded the Jerusalem Theater Workshop in 1967 and was long affiliated with the Khan Theater, also in Jerusalem. She was a Professor in the English Department at Hebrew University.

[13] **Righteous Among Nations,** an ongoing project Yad Vashem founded in 1963 to pay tribute to the non-Jews who risked their lives to save Jews from the Nazis. The process usually takes several years of extensive vetting: Atlan and her sisters were able to accelerate the process for their former nanny.

Poésie/Poetry

FROM

BONHEUR, MAIS SUR QUEL TON TE LE DIRE
HAPPINESS, BUT IN WHAT TONE TO TELL YOU

Atlan published six collections of poems in her lifetime, the first two, in 1961 and 1962, under the pseudonym Galil. Over the years, she habitually revised her texts, and included these rewritings in plays, prose works, or subsequent books of poetry. Passages from longer texts were occasionally separated into individual poems, though more often, individual poems became parts of longer texts. Atlan tended not to consider her books as discrete accomplishments, but, rather as related parts of an integral whole, arising from a common fount of experience and inspiration. Toward the end of her working life, Atlan returned to writing tightly compressed individual poems in both verse and prose.

    I strove to provide the strongest poems from every part of Atlan's working life. We include her final book in its entirety. Readers will notice that I changed the title; in the original it's *Peuples d'argile, Forêts d'étoiles* — literally *Peoples of Clay, Forests of Stars*.

La morte raconte

On distribuait des vêtements.
Je demandais le manteau sept, le manteau bleu. Personne ne l'avait demandé, ni reçu, il restait comme moi en souffrance, je nous sentais faits l'un pour l'autre. On me l'a accordé. Je voulais qu'on vérifie s'il était vraiment celui que je devais porter, si cette couleur bleue indiquait ma véritable destination. La couleur bleue est ma couleur d'enfance, mais j'aurais pris la rouge ou la noire ou la jaune, j'aurais pris l'abjection, la folie, le meurtre, s'ils m'étaient destinés. L'essentiel était de prendre la destination qui m'a vraiment été attribuée.

The Dead Woman Recounts

They were handing out garments.
I asked for coat seven, the blue coat.
No one else had requested, or received it, like me it was left hanging.
   I had the feeling
we'd been made for one another.
I wanted them to certify that this was the garment I was really
   supposed to wear,
if this blue was a sign of my true destination.
The color blue is my color of childhood, but I would have
   taken the red
or the black or the yellow, I would have taken abjection, madness,
   murder if they had been assigned.
It was crucial to take the destiny that was truly and specifically mine.

Le Maître des Marionnettes

Comme une Armoire ouvrez le Ciel
Où dort
Notre jouet le plus ancien
Le Maître des Marionnettes
Ombre des ombres
Robot de sable

Cassez le Ciel cette vitrine interminable

Dans une boîte de santal
Sur de la soie
Nous les coolies de l'ineffable
Rassemblerons Ta Face
Eparse

Tu nous a montré Ta Nuque Raide
Et Ton Stylet
Dans notre peau
Grava
Tes Lois de Fumée Noire.

Dansait le roi diseur de psaumes
Devant Ton arche
Remplie de Toi
De sable
Où brillaient des messages

The Master of Marionettes

Open the Sky as you would a Closet
Where our oldest plaything
The Master of Marionettes
Shadow of Shadows
Robot of sand
Is sleeping

Smash the Sky that endless window

In a sandalwood box
On silk
Coolies of the ineffable
We'll reassemble the fragments
Of Your Face

You showed us Your Stiff Neck
And your Stylus
Engraved
In our skin
Your Laws of Black Smoke.

The king, declaimer of psalms, danced
Before the Arc
That is suffused with Yourself
With the sand
Where messages glisten

Nous avons fait résonner Ton Nom dans le
désert des hommes
Nous avons trop porté Ton Nom et Ton
Etoile
A qui la faute si nous T'avons jeté avec nous
dans les flammes.

Maître des Marionnettes
Tourne Tes Noms vers la poussière
Ne Te révèle pas
Même à la poussière.

We have caused Your Name to echo in the
desert of men
For too long we carried Your Name and Your
Star
Whose fault is it if we flung You with ourselves
into the flames.

Master of Marionettes
Turn Your Names toward the dust
Do not Reveal Yourself
Even to the dust.

JE VOIS DES FLAMMES

Je vois des flammes.
Elles ne sont pas vraies.
Ce sont des restes de vraies flammes
Qui brûlent dans nos mémoires.

I See Flames

I see flames.
They're not real.
They're the remains of the real flames
That burn in our memory.

Tu es tout, tu n'es rien

Tu es tout, tu n'es rien, une servante vêtue de noir, qui se traverse elle-même comme un palais dont elle éteint toutes les lampes, une petite lumière tenue secrète, qui ne t'appartient pas, qui brillera même après toi.

You Are Everything, You Are Nothing

You are everything, you are nothing, a servant dressed in black, who wanders through herself as though in a palace where she douses all the lamps, a small secret light, which doesn't belong to you, which will shine even after you.

MÊME SEULE DANS SA MAISON ELLE SE SENTAIT HABITÉE

Elle avait remplacé l'anneau de son mariage par une bague, pour dire qu'elle restait mariée, à la terre, à la vie, de façon si intense que même seule dans sa maison elle se sentait traversée, habitée.

Even Alone in Her House She Felt Inhabited

She had replaced her wedding band with a ring, to declare that she remained married, to the earth, to life, and so intensely that even alone in her house she felt inhabited, suffused.

FROM

*QUELQUES PAGES ARRACHÉES AU
GRAND LIVRE DES RÊVES*

SOME PAGES TORN FROM THE
GREAT BOOK OF DREAMS

Le rêve de la salle d'études

Dans une salle d'études depuis longtemps déserte une voix prononce des mots anciens.
« DIEU » : Les femmes l'ont inventé.
Commentaire : Pour rabattre aux hommes leur caquet.
Ou encore : Parce-qu'elles sont faibles. De leur faiblesse est née l'idée de l'infini.
Ou encore : Parce-qu'elles sont mères. Pourquoi les mères ?...
Nous étudions ces paroles reçues en rêve, assis à de grandes tables, devant des cahiers couverts de nos écritures. Je me trouve à côté d'une très vieille femme, elle a passé sa vie à sauver des enfants qui n'étaient pas les siens, ils sont là autour d'elle, immatériels, lui donnant une aura infinie, comme un savoir non écrit rend inépuisables les paroles notées.

The Dream of the Study Hall

In a long-deserted study hall a voice pronounces ancient words.
"GOD": An invention of women.
Commentary: In order to bring men down a peg or two.
Or: Because women are weak. From their weakness, the idea of infinity was born.
Or: Because they are mothers. Why mothers? . . .
We studied these words which came to us in a dream, sitting at large tables, before notebooks covered with our writings. I am next to a very old woman, she spent her life saving children who were not her own, here they are, all around her, immaterial, giving her an aura of infinity, as a wisdom that's not inscribed makes written words inexhaustible.

Le rêve de l'étoile enfant

Un homme très grand, très corpulent, marchait, précédé par sa propre tête, on sentait qu'il veillait sur elle comme un père attentif à laisser libre son enfant qui marche pour la première fois, tout en restant prêt à l'aider s'il tombait, des personnes de plus en plus nombreuses l'accompagnaient, tendues vers le ciel, la tête roulait, peu à peu ronde, étoile naissante portée de loin par ses nombreux parents.

The Dream of the Star-Child

A very tall, very corpulent man was walking preceded by his own head, he seemed a father watching over his child, wanting him to be free as he took his first steps, but ready to assist if he should fall, in ever greater numbers people arrived to accompany them in a line stretching toward the sky, the head rolled, little by little becoming round, a nascent star brought from afar by its numerous parents.

Le rêve de l'oubli

Nous nous trouvons sur la plus haute des montagnes, au tout début de l'univers. Un homme, si grand que sa tête touche le ciel, murmure : « Le mythe de la naissance et celui de la mort sont si cruels que nous les oublierons. » Nous les oublions. Nous limitons nos regards, ne souffrant de la chute infinie d'où surgit l'univers que la peine actuelle. Nous dévalons les pentes, de montagne en montagne, la neige devient grise, parsemée de charognes, rien n'arrête la descente acharnée de notre peloton. Soudain, dans un éclair, nous ne pouvons pas ne pas voir dans quelle chute irréversible nous entraîne cette force d'où surgit l'univers. Quelqu'un crie, meurt dans nos bras. Nous l'oublions. Nous ne pensons qu'à suivre le Peloton, absorbés dans le confortable effort de ne souffrir que la peine actuelle.

The Dream of Oblivion

We are on the highest of all mountains, at the very beginning of the universe. A man, so tall that his head touches the sky, murmurs: "The myths of birth and death are so cruel that we shall forget them." We forget them. We limit where we look, in the infinite fall from which the universe surged we suffer only present pain. We go tumbling down from the peaks, from mountain to mountain, the snow turns gray, strewn with carcasses, nothing stops the relentless descent of our pack. Suddenly, there's a flash of lightning, we can't help but see that the force from which the universe surged has trapped us in this irreversible fall. Someone screams, dies in our arms. We forget. We think only of following the Pack, absorbed in the comfortable effort of suffering only present pain.

Le rêve des bols pleins de lumière

Je me trouvais dans une rue bordée de maisons très belles, construites à l'envers. J'entrais dans l'une d'elles, des gens allaient, venaient, la tête plongée dans les bols, inondés de lumière. Sous leurs pas des flammes prenaient, la pièce allait brûler, ils enfonçaient d'autant plus fort leur tête dans les bols. Le feu est déclaré, ils ont déménagé, à nouveau des flammes sortent du plancher, ils les ignorent, ils vont et viennent, illuminés.

The Dream of the Bowls Full of Light

I found myself in a street lined with very beautiful houses, built upside down. I entered one, people came and went, their heads plunged in bowls flooded with light. Beneath their feet, flames were catching, the room was going to burn, they buried their heads even more deeply in their bowls. The fire broke out, they moved on, flames again broke through the floor, oblivious they came and went, illuminated.

Le rêve des mains

J'étais dans une forêt faite de mains blanches et fines. Je voyais une grande pierre fendue en deux par un sourire. Ce qu'il restait d'une femme évanouie d'aimer. Lèvres et mains si belles que la lumière les sculptait.

The Dream of the Hands

I was in a forest made of fine, white hands. I saw a great rock split in two by a smile. The remains of a woman who faded away from loving. Lips and hands so beautiful that the light was sculpting them.

Le rêve des bébés

On trempait des bébés dans du lait, on les faisait dorer, on les étalait sur des présentoirs, les clients affluaient, la consommation de bébés croustillants ne cessait d'augmenter, les actionnaires de la Multinationale « Les Savoureux » se régalaient et prospérait.

The Dream of Babies

They dipped babies in milk, they gilded them, they arranged them on display counters, customers came flooding in, the consumption of crispy babies did nothing but rise, shareholders of the multinational "Delectable, Inc." were delighted and made a fortune.

Le rêve du torrent de lumière

Je me trouvais dans le métro, soudain, un torrent de lumière m'emportait, il n'était pas plus large que mon corps, il tournait brusquement sur lui-même, me pliant, me tordant, je ne m'inquiétais pas, je savais que j'avais retrouvé mon élément natal.

THE DREAM OF THE TORRENT OF LIGHT

I was in the metro, suddenly a torrent of light carried me away, it was no larger than my own body, it curled around itself, folding me, twisting me, I wasn't afraid, I knew that I'd found my native element.

Le rêve de la morte fatiguée d'être seule

Je me reposais dans ma chambre, une femme essayait d'entrer, la peau de son visage était lisse, bleutée, elle n'avait ni yeux ni lèvres, elle n'était qu'une force douée d'un corps, une force d'une extrême violence, je pesais sur la porte de tout mon poids pour l'empêcher d'entrer, elle finit par l'ouvrir, je la reconnus, elle était ma grand-mère lorsqu'elle était vivante, comme enterrée dans sa maison à force d'être seule, je la repousse, j'ai pitié d'elle, elle vient me chercher pour que je lui tienne compagnie dans sa tombe.

The Dream of the Dead Woman Tired of Being Alone

I was resting in my bedroom, a woman was trying to come in, the skin of her face was smooth, bluish, she had no eyes or lips, she was nothing but a force endowed with a body, a force of extreme violence, I leaned with all my weight against the door, but she managed to burst in, I recognized her, she was my grandmother when she was alive, as though buried in her house from the force of being alone, I'm pushing her away, I pity her, she's come to get me to keep her company in her tomb.

FROM
LE MAÎTRE-MUR
THE MASTER-WALL

(FROM THE NOTEBOOKS
OF MY PREHISTORY)

Les rats en fête sur l'autel

Aux fêtes du pardon
Je rôde
Cherchant la porte
Parmi les cendres

Les rats en fête
Sur l'autel
Grignotent
Le rideau bleu du tabernacle

À qui la faute
Si tu dors
Sur une terre
Qui te hait

Rats Feasting on the Altar

At the feasts of forgiveness
I prowl
Searching for the door
Among the ashes

Rats feasting
On the altar
Nibble
The blue curtain of the tabernacle

Who is at fault
If you sleep
On an earth
That hates you

J'AI VU LA MORT PLEURER

J'ai vu la mort pleurer
Au soleil
Sur un banc

Elle cousait
De ses doigts lents
Une chemise de fil blanc

Les enfants la portaient sur la pelouse aux cyclones
Leurs mains devenaient blanches
La mort leur souriait de loin sur ses béquilles
Des chiens portaient sa laine et lui trouvaient des bancs

Pour toi qu'elle a aimé tant malhabile
Monde qui cherche en vain dans le monde un asile
Elle a cousu, de ses vieux doigts fragiles
Une maison d'étoile et de vêtements blancs

I Saw Death Weeping

I saw death weeping
On a bench
In the sun

She was sewing
With her slow fingers
A shirt of white thread

Children carried her over the lawn to the cyclones
Their hands turning white
Death smiled at them from a distance leaning on her crutches
Dogs carried her wool and found her benches

For you whom she loved with such a clumsy love
World vainly searching in the world for asylum
She sewed, with her old fragile fingers
A house of stars and white vestments

La petite voiture de flammes et de voix

J'ouvrais la fenêtre, au lieu de la baie j'apercevais un château absolument désert, aux arbres rasés, aux allées maniaques.

Une petite voiture de flammes qui ne brûlaient pas — ce n'était qu'un morceau de soleil couchant — avançait sans rouler ni voler lentement.

Les miens m'enfonçaient la tête dans un sac pour m'étouffer, ils appuyaient sur mes poignets et mes chevilles, les broyaient et je hurlai.

J'étais absolument déserte. Cela n'empêchait pas qu'on me tordait, qu'on m'asphyxiait. Et les voix pullulaient, coassaient. J'étais chez moi, à l'étranger, hôtel, avec des dettes à payer, d'une autre vie. Le garçon nettoyait le hall, il raclait le tapis, la poussière collait, il dut racler jusqu'aux assises, tout arracher.

J'étais dans un théâtre dont les ouvreuses à peu près nues flambaient. C'était l'avant-garde la plus récente et les critiques s'extasiaient.

Je ne bougeais pas de chez moi et j'avais le sentiment d'être de plus en plus à l'étranger. Les lettres qu'on m'envoyait, d'avant, ouvertes, sur les buffets, régnaient. Déjà bien isolée, ma maison de plus en plus enfonçait, se retirait, je la retenais, j'esssayais, il ne resta bientôt qu'un chemin de chèvre qui pût me relier.

The Chariot of Flames and Voices

I was opening the window, instead of the bay I perceived a castle that was totally wrecked, its trees razed, its paths maniacal.

A small chariot of flames that didn't burn — a slice of the setting sun — advanced slowly without flying or rolling.

My family forced my head into a sack so I couldn't breathe, they leaned on my wrists and ankles, pounding, I screamed.

I was absolutely done in. Which didn't stop them from wrenching and smothering me. The croaking voices proliferated. I stayed home, away, hotel, with debts to pay from another life. An employee was cleaning the hall, scraping the carpet, the dust stuck to the carpet, to get it all out, he had to scrape down to the floor.

I was in a theatre where the usherettes, basically naked, were on fire. It was the latest of the avant-garde, and the critics were ecstatic.

I stayed home but more and more I had the feeling that I was in a foreign country. Letters I'd received, from before, lay open, crowning the tabletops. My house, already isolated, was sinking into itself, withdrawing, I held on, I kept trying, soon there would be only a goat path that could keep me connected.

Peuples d'argile, forêts d'étoiles
As One Would Chisel Diamonds (2000)

La lumière éclaire l'abîme,
l'abîme rend bouleversante la
lumière.

Light lets us see the abyss,
the abyss renders light unbearable.

L'EAU DE MÉMOIRE

Princes, je vous convie.
Ce soir je donne un grand festin.
Une soirée de long silence
Où nous boirons l'eau de mémoire.

Sur la cordée d'un même songe,
De Pythagore à Galilée,
Une pléiade obscure longe
La ville morte illuminée.

Les serviteurs portent les jarres.
Princes du monde, elles sont vides.
La belle et fabuleuse histoire
A froid dans les lumiéres de la ville.

Interrogez la peine immense
De ces diseurs de verité.
Princes, buvez l'eau de mémoire.
Ouvrez la porte aux Étrangers.

The Water of Memory

High Princes, I invite you.
Tonight I offer a great feast,
an evening of long silence
so we may drink the water of memory.

Linked in a single dream
From Pythagoras to Galileo,
A dark cluster of stars
Borders the shining dead city.

Servants carry in the vessels.
High Princes, they are empty.
Our fabled and beautiful history
lies freezing in the lights of the city.

Question the great pain
Of these tellers of truths.
High Princes, drink the water of memory
Open your door to Strangers.

Forêts d'étoiles

Les soirs de pleine lune et de forêts d'étoiles
Rêvaient de longs vieillards sur leur vieux livre aimé
Où leur dieu leur parlait dans sa langue scellée

Dans leur cabane au toit de feuillage et de ciel
Ils percevaient l'écho du chant des survivants
Quand la terre a cessé de trembler

Quand la lune était rouge et les étoiles noires
Les vieillards se taisaient plutôt que de lui dire
Ce qu'ils n'osaient penser

Ils chantaient sa louange avec une ferveur
Sauvage et la plainte emmurée
Dans leur coeur ils ne l'entendaient pas

Quand des mères dont les enfants venaient d'être jetés
vivants dans les flames hurlaient
Ils priaient avec une ferveur encore plus farouche

Les soirs de pleine lune et de forêts d'étoiles
Les vieillards laissaient parler leur coeur et blessés
Lui pardonnaient l'Histoire.

Star Forests

Nights of star forests and the full moon
ancient old men dreamed on their beloved book
where they could hear the hermetic language of their god

In their hut with its roof of leaves and sky
they sensed the echo of survivors singing
from when the earth had ceased to tremble

When the moon was red and the stars were black
the old men fell silent, they could not tell him
what they dared not think

They chanted his praises
with wild zeal but could not hear
the moaning smothered in their heart

As mothers screamed to see their children
thrown living into the flames
they prayed with even wilder devotion

Nights of star forests and the full moon
the old men allowed their hearts to speak,
and, wounded, absolved Him of History.

La douleur anonyme au soleil rayonnait

Une montagne en bois entièrement cirée,
sculptée,
surgissait,
un torrent de têtes
déchiquetées
la balafrait,
le cri éternel des morts devenant de la terre
n'était plus que tourment du relief,
la douleur anonyme au soleil rayonnait.

The Anonymous Sorrow Shining on the Sun

A carved and highly polished wooden mountain
was rising up
scarred by
a torrent of
battered heads,
the eternal cry of the dead become earth
no more than a crazed landscape
anonymous sorrow shining toward the sun.

Constat

Un être fabuleux gît en nous, à la longue altéré comme les épreuves d'un livre que l'on aurait oublié d'imprimer.

Based on the Evidence

A wondrous being lives within us, timeworn
like the proofs of a book
no one could remember to print.

TOUT SERA COMME ICI MAIS CE SERA VIVABLE

Là-bas, tout sera comme ici mais ce sera
vivable.
La grande migration commence.
Solennels nous traversons nos chambres.
Nous traversons les mers.
Nous nous perdons dans un désert
interminable.
Nous endurons la faim.
La soif.
La folie.
Là-bas –
Savons-nous même encore où nous voulons
aller
Tout sera comme ici mais ce sera vivable.
Ces mots
nous les chantons lorsque nous sommes gais
lorsque nous some désespérés
lorsque nous sommes à bout de forces:
Là-bas – tout sera –
comme – ici – mais – ce – sera – vivable.

Everything Will Be Like Here but It Will Be Livable

Everything there will be like here
but it will be livable.
The great migration begins.
Solemn, we cross our rooms.
We cross the seas.
We lose our way in a desert
without end.
We endure hunger.
Thirst.
Madness.
There--
We still know where we want
to go
Everything will be like here but it will be livable.
These words--
we sing them when we're glad
when we despair
when we're at the end of our strength:
Then – everything will be –
like – here – but – it – will – be – livable.

Le tram qui s'effritait

Je me trouvais dans un tram fait de terre, il peinait sur des pentes abruptes qui donnaient sur des gouffres, il ne s'arrêtait nulle part, il ne transportait que moi, il s'effritait, il ne restait plus rien de lui lorsqu'il m'abandonna, je me trouvais près d'une sorte de refuge perdu au milieu d'étendues vides.

THE TRAM THAT CRUMBLED AWAY

I was in a tram made of earth, which struggled on the steep slopes above the void, not stopping, transporting no one but me, crumbling away to nothing by the time it abandoned me, near a sort of haven lost in a vast emptiness.

Au milieu d'une foule oubliée

Je voyais des montagnes de poupées en porcelain perdues dans une eau méchante et claire, au milieu de leur foule, oubliée, j'appelais, j'appelais.

In the Middle of a Forgotten Heap

I saw mountains of porcelain dolls lost in clear malevolent waters, in the middle of their heap, unremembered, I called, I called.

Le temps que je crie au miracle

Des vagues, haineuses, me dévisageaient. Une paysanne, de ses mains nues, les écartait, elle les maintenait dresseés vers le ciel le temps que je crie au miracle, puis elle les laissait devenir des serpents.

While I Called Out for a Miracle

Waves, hateful waves, were staring through me. With her bare hands, a peasant woman parted them, held them up toward the sky while I called out for a miracle, then she let them become snakes.

Le bracelet de la lumière noire

Je marchais dans la mer aidée d'un grand bâton, autour de moi des monceaux d'êtres se laissaient couler, je fus bientôt seule au milieu de cette eau, à la longue elle s'ouvrit sur une vallée claire où des arbres dorés tintaient, leurs sons et leurs parfums réveillaient je ne sais quelle joie enfermée dans mes veines, j'en oubliais ce bracelet de lumière noire gravé à l'intérieur de mon poignet, où l'heure de ma mort est sans cesse avancée.

The Bracelet of Black Light

I was walking in the sea with the aid of a big stick, all around me heaps of living beings let themselves sink, presently I was alone in the middle of these waters, which finally opened on a shining valley where golden trees were chiming, their sounds and perfumes rousing the ineffable joy imprisoned in my veins, I forgot this bracelet of black light engraved on my inner wrist, which ceaselessly clocks the coming hour of my death.

Ces travaux que l'on fait dans mon coeur

Terreur de naître.
Terreur première.
Terreur Mère.
Oubliée.
Ravivée.
Par ces travaux que l'on fait dans mon coeur.
Par la terreur d'avoir à naître une deuxième fois.

These Labors Imposed on My Heart

Birth terror
First terror
Mother terror
Forgotten
Again begotten
in these labors imposed on my heart
in terror of having to be re-birthed.

* * *

... J'ai traversé les zones noires de la résurrection ...

* * *

. . . I have crossed the black zones of resurrection . . .

La lumière oubliée de nos premières heures

Je voyais se dresser devant mes yeux fermés des serpents noirs déchiquetés, ils se succédaient par flots de plus en plus menaçants et serrés, ils tombaient vers moi terrifiés, mon corps m'avertissait, il couvait ma mort, au bout de longues heures d'une douleur telle que je croyais ne plus pouvoir la supporter les serpents s'effilochèrent, ils devenaient des flots de formes noires moins torturées, soudain ils fusèrent, en gerbes de lumière, la lumière oubliée de nos premières heures.

The Forgotten Light of Our First Hours

My eyes closed, I saw battered black snakes rising up, wave upon wave, ever more threatening and dense, in terror the snakes tumbled toward me, my body let me know it was brooding my death, after long hours of bearing a pain I could bear no longer, the snakes fell to pieces, they formed less tortured black waves, suddenly they fused, in sprays of light, the forgotten light of our first hours.

JE PORTE UN PRÉNOM DE POUSSIÈRE

Je porte un prénom de poussière.
Fleur et poussière.
Sable et or.
Vêtements éphémères.

I Bear a Name Made of Dust

I bear a name made of dust
Flowers and dust.
Sand and gold.
Ephemeral vestments.

Celui dont je garde le nom secret

Celui dont je garde le nom secret venait vers moi, j'allais vers lui, une femme surgissait, il m'oubliait, ils s'enlaçaient, avec un tel amour, surgi de la source unique de leurs deux êtres, il avait dû traverser leur vie, il les irriguait de lumière à la fin de leur vie.

HE WHOSE NAME I KEEP SECRET

He whose name I keep secret was coming toward me, I was going toward him, suddenly a woman appeared, he forgot all about me, they embraced, with a love that flowed from the singular source of their beings, a love that must have streamed through their lives, bathing them with light at the end of their lives.

Le scintillement du sable à l'infini

Pour toi,
l'amour,
le vrai,
qui traverse ta vie.

Pour moi,
le désert, ses oasis,
leur beauté noire et leur mélancolie,
le scintillement du sable à l'infini.

The Sparkle of Sand for Eternity

For you
true love
and life
in unity.

For me
the desert and its oases,
their dolor and dark beauty,
the sparkle of sand for eternity.

* * *

On ne peut vivre seul on ne peut vivre inhabité

* * *

One cannot live alone one cannot live uninhabited

MA MORT ET MOI: CHANSON

Ma mort et moi nous déjeunons ensemble
Nous dînons ensemble
Nous nous couchons
Nous nous levons ensemble

Nous ne nous quittons pas
Nous ne nous parlons pas
Nous ne nous aimons pas
Nous ne nous voyons pas

Je ne pense qu'à elle
Elle est née avec moi
Elle disparaîtra en même temps que moi
Elle est née pour moi

Elle était là, dans ma mère
avec moi
Elle a veillé sur mon berceau
elle a veillé sur mon enfance

Elle me protège
sans défaillance
dès que j'aime
dès que je vis elle m'en prive

Elle aime la poésie
Elle s'en nourrit

My Death and I: A Song

My death and I have lunch together
We sup together
We go to bed
We get up together

We don't leave each other
We don't speak to each other
We don't love each other
We don't see each other

I think only of her
She was born with me
She'll disappear with me
She was born for me

She was with me in my mother
She guarded my cradle
she guarded my youth

She protects me
like an iron glove
She lets me live
but forbids me love

She loves poetry
consumes poetry

Elle en a une faim
insatiable

Elle veut que j'écrive
que je ne vive
que pour cela
écrire

Et moi je rêve
d'aimer un être
et d'être sienne
et d'être sienne

S'il me rejoint
ma mort l'éloigne
s'il lui résiste elle me force
à l'éloigner de moi

Elle veut
pour elle seule
mon sang
ma force vive

in mad binges
but cannot be satisfied

She wants me to write
in order to live
And only to write
does she want me to live

And I dream
of a living lover
and that I am his very own
and that I am his very own

If he should come to me
my death will hold him at bay
If he resists she will force me
to send him away

For herself alone
she wants
my blood
my vital energy

TU ME RENDAIS VIVANTE

Tout prend fin
lorsque cela commence
lorsqu'enfin si tard
tu me rendais vivante.

Tes mains me manquent
Tes mains de musicien qui jouaient de mon corps
lié au tien si profondément
qu'il devenait mon âme.

You Brought Me Back to Life

It all begins to end
when it begins
when finally and so late
you brought me back to life.

I miss your hands
your musician's hands that played my body
which so harmonized with yours
that your body became my soul.

Le dire sur le ton d'une douleur gaie

Vivante. Au passé. Le dire sur le ton d'une douleur gaie, d'une gaieté drôle, précieuse comme un parapet qui protège de tomber dans le vide.

Tell It with a Joking Sorrow

So full of life. Indeed she was. Tell it with a joking sorrow, a queer joke precious as the parapet that protects us from the void.

Le châle des fins de vie

Sur ma personne ralentie,
lassée,
je mets mon châle des fins de vie.

C'est un châle aux couleurs raffinées,
discrètes,
assourdies.

Je le portais au cimetière
quand j'ai jeté sur ma petite soeur
quelques poignées de terre.

Je le porte dès que je me sens seule,
dans la rue, dans la maison,
chez mes amis.

Il me tient compagnie.
Il me rend invisible.
C'est un châle qui s'accorde avec les fins de vie.

Shawl for the Ends of Life

On these weary bones that
have weathered their share of strife,
I drape my shawl for the ends of life.

Refined, discreet, and muted
are the colors of this shawl.

I wore it to the graveyard
when I threw clumps of earth
on my little sister.

I wear it whenever I feel alone,
in the street, when I'm at home,
when I leave to make a social call.

It keeps me company, does my shawl.
It renders me invisible.
Perfect for the ends of life, is my shawl.

SI LA RÉSURRECTION DES MORTS N'EST PAS UN CANULAR

Si la résurrection des morts n'est pas un canular, dès que nous nous réveillerons nos débris chercheront les débris des êtres que nous avions aimés.

De nos voix réduites au silence nous crierons notre douleur ancienne plus vive que jamais, notre douleur d'aimer, de ne pas être aimés.

Nous ne penserons qu'à régler nos vieux comptes, pourquoi avais-tu réfusé de m'épouser, avec qui m'avais tu trompé(e), pourquoi m'as-tu abandonné(e)?

Et ce cri déchirera même le coeur des pierres: Pourquoi tes restes ne veulent-ils pas des miens?

Les passants s'étonneront de cette clameur sauvage, drôle, style boulevard, qui montera des tombes!

If the Resurrection of the Dead Is Not a Scam

If the resurrection of the dead is not a scam,
as soon as we awaken our remains will go
looking for the remains of those we loved.

In voices stripped of sound we'll shriek
with the ancient agony that's more alive than ever,
the agony of loving, of having never been loved.

Our minds will obsess on old accounts:
why did you refuse to marry me?
why did you cheat and with whom?
why did you abandon me?

Why don't your bones want my bones?
A cry to rend the heart of stones.

Passersby will be amazed by the clamor—
the brutal boulevard theatrics—
bursting from the tombs!

L'ÉTUDE

Je me trouvais dans un salon, on me poussait, avec beaucoup d'égards, dans le coin réservé à ceux dont le nom figure sur la liste rouge, celle que de ses propres mains la Mort établit.

On me transférait dans des couloirs de plus en plus aigus, étroits. Rien de mauvais n'arrivait. J'étais en attente. Aucun espoir, mais en attente.

L'ÉTUDE. Le mot ne fut pas prononcé, ce n'était pas la peine, il était là, inscrit, en lettres vives, dans mon coeur. Inscrit et oublié. Étudier. Ni pour guérir, ni pour gagner de temps. Pour l'étude elle-même. Pour qu'elle vive.

Study

I found myself in a large sitting room, I was being pushed, with great respect, to the corner reserved for those whose names were on the red list, drawn up by the very hands of Death.

I was ushered down corridors that were increasingly narrow, tight. Nothing bad was happening. I was in a state of waiting. No hope at all. Waiting.

STUDY. The word was not pronounced, there was no need, it was there, inscribed in living letters, on my heart. Inscribed and forgotten. Study. Not in order to be healed, or to gain time. But for the sake of study. So that our learning shall live.

Le rêve de l'hôtel des morts

Je me trouvais dans une chambre d'hôtel assise par terre en face d'un ami mort récemment, il écrivait des poèmes comme il l'a toujours fait, un autre se droguait comme avant de s'être suicidé, une femme attendait son amant, un enfant pleurait, j'écoutais les nouvelles, inquiète pour les miens, pour moi-même, oubliant que j'étais déjà morte.

Hotel for the Dead: A Dream

I was in a hotel room, sitting on the floor across from a friend who had recently died, he was writing poems as he'd always done, another was taking drugs like before he committed suicide, a woman was tending to her lover, a child was crying, I was listening to the news, worried for my family, for myself, forgetting that I was already dead.

Peuples d'argile

Je voyais des êtres se métamorphoser, ils étaient morts mais quelque chose les travaillait, peut-être étaient-ils de l'argile sculptée par une main qui ne se montrait pas, une main faite de leur propre chair qui n'en finit pas de se recommencer.

People of Clay

I kept seeing the metamorphosis of certain beings, they were dead but something was molding them, perhaps they were made of clay, sculpted by a hand that wouldn't reveal itself, a hand forged of their own flesh which kept starting all over again.

Le son de l'âme qui me traverse

Je dessine au soleil des idoles que je n'ai jamais vues, elles naissent de mes mains désoeuvrées, d'une prière involontaire émanée d'une zone de mon être où même en rêve je ne pénètre pas. Je ne connais pas le son de l'âme qui me traverse.

THE SOUND OF THE SOUL PASSING THROUGH ME

In the sunlight I draw idols that I have never seen, they are born of my empty hands, arise from a prayer unconsciously issued forth from a zone of my being or even from a dream I cannot penetrate. I don't recognize the sound of the soul passing through me.

COMME ON CISÈLERAIT DES DIAMANTS

Écrire comme on cisèlerait des diamants tout en m'enfonçant lentement dans la terre.

De tout mon être défaillant, remonter l'échelle de mes âmes jusqu'à leur source la plus haute, l'abîme d'où la lumière naît, la lumière d'où l'abîme renaît.

La lumière éclaire l'abîme, l'abîme rend bouleversante la lumière.

As One Would Chisel Diamonds

To write as one would chisel diamonds,
even as I sink slowly into the earth.

With my whole faltering being, to re-climb
the ladder of my souls to their highest source,
the abyss that births the light, the light
that engenders the abyss.

Light lets us see the abyss, the abyss
renders light unbearable.

ADIEU POSTHUME DE LILIANE
LILIANE'S POSTHUMOUS ADIEU

Morte, je parle, à tous mes amis

Mes amis, mes chers amis, bien que je sois
morte, je vous parle.
Faites-moi l'amitié de m'écouter.
Je vous parle en silence car je n'ai plus de voix.
Je suis enfoulée dans cette boîte que vous
venez de mettre dans la terre.
Vous me pleurez, je vous en remercie.
Je vis encore un peu grâce à votre amitié.
Je vous dis, vous re-dis, en silence comme
je vous aimais...
quand, même morts, nous ne pouvons
cesser...
de nous...
aimer...

Dead, I speak, to all my friends

My friends, my dear friends, though I am
dead, I speak to you.
Be so tender as to listen.
I speak to you in silence for I no longer have a voice.
I am buried in this box that you
have placed in the earth.
I am grateful that you weep for me.
In the grace of your friendship,
I live a little longer.
I say, and say again, in silence, how much
I loved you...
for, even dead, we do not
cease...
to love...
one another...

On Translating Liliane Atlan

A Conversation between Marguerite Feitlowitz and Merrill Leffler

In your introduction, you write that Liliane's "writing is steeped in her learned agon with Torah, Talmud, and Kabbalah, and her French is inflected with Hebrew, Ladino, and Yiddish." Did you have to take such allusions or usages into account?

This was particularly important when I was translating Liliane's plays, *The Carriage of Flames and Voices, The Messiahs,* and *Mr. Fugue. The Carriage of Flames and Voices* is built on the schema of Merkabah mysticism, which has its roots in the 6th century BCE writings of the prophet Ezekiel. Living in exile in Babylonia after the destruction of Jerusalem in 586 BCE, he had a vision of a "throne-chariot" (God's throne), which inspired and emboldened him both to warn his people of impending danger and to prophesy that ultimately they would be saved, redeemed. It was Bettina Knapp who guided me in this area, for I had little background at the time; needless to say, I studied Gershom Scholem's *Kabbalah* and *Major Trends in Jewish Mysticism*. What Liliane did in her dramatic writing was extraordinary: having internalized the canonical and mystical texts from her own years of study and practice, she somehow rendered the ancient imagery immediate, inseparable from the horrors of the Holocaust, yet mysterious and embedded in the warring psyches of her main character, who is literally a split, or double, human being. The play is a poem, intensely musical and mysterious. Deeply personal and surreal, yet one with Jewish foundational history and law, rational thought, wonder, and awe.

The presence of Hebrew, Ladino and Yiddish are in the cadences and tonalities. Yiddish I had in my ear from my paternal relatives. I'd also studied Ladino while I was living in Spain and then in New York; I'm far from an expert, but it's been an interest of mine.

When you translated Liliane's three plays, you worked with her. Was she critical, in a literary sense, of some of your translation choices? Did this make you more aware of choices you went on to make in translating the poetry?

This was my first book, and it was thrilling to work with Liliane. Before she arrived in New York, I'd been meeting several times a week with Bettina Knapp — Betinna was a prolific scholar of French literature, especially theater. She and I would go over every line together at the breakfasts she would prepare for me in her beautiful Upper West Side apartment. These meetings were a whole education for me, not least because Bettina, who was born in France and wholly bilingual, encouraged me to trust my ear, to let the texts seep into me viscerally. We read every line aloud, often multiple times, switching back and forth so we could each both read and listen. Liliane and I would do the same thing later on in my much more modest Brooklyn apartment. I'm not sure that Liliane actually liked English as a language — she certainly recognized its literary history and power, vast vocabulary, and active verbs, but French was the linguistic love of her life. She trusted me when it came to English, and though we had long, involved analyses of word choices, she never imposed a choice or registered the kind of skepticism that could have shut me down. That I had Bettina's imprimatur was, I think, very important. In her work with me, it was writer to writer; she took the opportunity of my translations to revise her original texts and had me translate the new passages. I have to say, this still rather amazes me; I was so young (in my twenties), and it was my first book.

Was there a difference for you in translating the poems, compared with translating the plays, e.g., dialogue?

The dialogue in Liliane's plays tends not to be straightforward, or "the way we really speak." To take one example in *The Carriage of Flames and Voices*, the language, as I noted above, is often surreal, even when the voices sound very "down to earth," bantering, bickering, and complaining. The language of *Mister Fugue* is full of both cruelty and the heartbreaking tenderness among characters — children — who have lost any shred of illusion that they will survive and yet act out the lives they would have led into old age. *The Messiahs* — who include Moses, The Eye, Grumbling Mummy, and Radio — play with canonical language in ways that call into question blasphemy, faith, tradition, history, and the odds of redemption, while stranded on their own planet. There is poetry in Liliane's plays and drama in her poems; her narratives are composed of vignettes with multiple characters navigating odd situations. I think that my having spent so much time with Liliane, who was a wonderful mimic and *raconteuse*, was also helpful.

I don't think you worked with Liliane in translating her poems — are there poems that had special challenges for you? Was Liliane's "voice," so to speak, in your head?

Liliane's voice(s) were certainly in my mind. Each poem offers its own challenges. To take one example, "My Death and I: A Song" ("Ma morte et moi: chanson"), pp. 122-125: the poem absolutely had to be a *song*, with a lilting rhythm and palpable subtext of mixed emotions. The prose poems in the section, "Some Pages Torn from the Great Book of Dreams," offer no explanation in the original — the strange visions are alive, absolute — and my job was to render them with utter clarity. Readers will notice that I changed the title of her final book: in the original it is *Peuples d'argile, forêts d'étoiles* — literally "Peoples of Clay, Forests of Stars." For me, it just isn't as haunting or evocative in the English; and

I wanted a title that better embraced the whole volume, so I chose "As One Would Chisel Diamonds" ("*Comme on cisèlerait des diamants*"), one of her very last poems.

There are poems where you've translated or made adjustments for the spirit of the French, not a word-for-word literal — can you give an example?

In "The Sparkle of Sands for Eternity" ("Le scintillement du sable à l'infini"), pp. 118-119, I made a change that will be obvious to readers who have French. Liliane's first stanza is: "Pour toi,/ l'amour / le vrai / qui traverse ta vie." A French reader will also see that this small poem is actually quite rich in rhyme: "vie," the last word in the first stanza rhymes with the last words of the final two lines of the second stanza, "mélancholie" and "l'infini." I felt this rhyme was essential to the entire poem — it lends music and keeps the narrator bound, in a sense, with a lover who has moved on. So I recast the first stanza: "For you / true love / and life / in unity." I haven't strayed from the meaning, but I have certainly used different words. In "Shawl for the Ends of Life" ("Le châle des fins de vie"), pp. 130-131, I made a different sort of re-arrangement. Readers will note that the second stanza in the French has three lines, and that the English has two. In the French, there are rhymes among the adjectives that follow their respective nouns, between the first and second stanzas ("lassée/raffinées" and "ralentie/vie/ assourdies"). English being less rhyme rich than French, I chose rhythm over rhyme. (The strong final stop in the French second stanza was very helpful in creating an English cadence.) In English, the adjective almost always must precede the noun, and so I wrote: "Refined, discreet, and muted / are the colors of this shawl," setting up a later rhyme with "call" and the final two repetitions of "shawl." This all sounds very technical, I know, but it was in service to the songlike quality that is essential to this beautiful poem, and my adjectives are very close to the French.

How did translating Liliane's poetry differ from other French writers you've translated?

Let me approach this question from a wider angle: I translate Spanish-language poets, playwrights, and prose writers as well. I've always been attracted to writers whose styles are very different from my own; I like the opportunity to stretch or contract, as the case might be, to have new points of reference, and new challenges, new "clay" to work with, if you will. Griselda Gambaro also writes surreal and searing plays steeped in history; but the theatrics are totally different from Liliane's; Chilean poet Ennio Moltedo writes prose poems that are taut, very political, and often surreal. Luisa Valenzuela writes in a myriad of voices and styles, and is often as funny as she is frightening. As part of my apprenticeship, I translated Léopold Sédar Senghor, Aimé Césaire, René Depestre, and Mohammad Dib — francophone writers who very deliberately bent and stretched, really re-invented literary French. My immersion in those writers had to have had their role in preparing me for Liliane's work.

Is there a process you have in translating a body of poetry such as Liliane's? What are you "going for" as far as sound, rhythms, images, and meaning are concerned?

Well, of course, I'm "going for" it all! But one does have to make choices — in a given text, one might need to prioritize rhyme; or cadence as opposed to rhyme; or alliterations that follow patterns different from those in the original. It may sound paradoxical, but one makes changes in order to stay closer to the original. Translation is an act of *writing* — and this writing is the fruit of the particular reading(s) of a particular translator at a particular moment in their life, and in the history of the world. There must be originality in translating, if there is not, then the result is slavish, and the vitality of the original is squelched.

I have made a practice of translating fairly large bodies of work from each of my chosen authors — I'm attracted to immersion, to living with texts and oeuvres for a long time. Writers have histories and habits, patterns and obsessions and quirks, and getting a feel for these is essential. Immersion hones our intuition, activates associations we might otherwise not have, gives us the time to develop the verbal skills called for in the originals. I don't have a hard-and-fast process; I want the membrane between me and the text to be as porous as possible.

Are there poems in which you might have had alternative translations, e.g., diction, sound, rhythm?

I tend to make my first drafts quite quickly, but at the same time, I like to note alternatives and possibilities. There's no need to make abiding commitments so early in the process. Sometimes, a translation just comes like a gift, with little to do in the way of revision. But that's the exception! G-d, they say, is in the details, which may be true — what's *certainly* true is that our choices in the details will make or break the translation.

Translator's Acknowledgments

For their generosity, warmth, and expert care of their mother's literary legacy, we extend special thanks to Michaël Atlan and Miri Keren. They maintain a multi-lingual website about her work and life at www.lilianeatlan.com. My gratitude goes out to Julia Carpenter and Veronica Jorgensen for invaluable help with manuscript preparation; to David Anderson for his comments on multiple drafts of these translations; to Barbara Goldberg for introducing this project to Merrill Leffler, and to Merrill for his attention to small details on late versions, and for introducing me to the work of Mindy Weisel; and to Sandy Rodgers, my thanks for her beautiful design. Sandy and Mindy make this book a feast for the eyes.